S Mary L.
Dept. of Religious Studies

Attitudes to Nature

THEMES IN RELIGIOUS STUDIES SERIES

Series Editors: Jean Holm, with John Bowker

Other titles

Worship
Making Moral Decisions
Myth and History
Human Nature and Destiny
Picturing God
Rites of Passage
Women in Religion
Sacred Writings
Sacred Place

Attitudes to Nature

Edited by

Jean Holm

with John Bowker

PINTER
PUBLISHERS
LONDON, NEW YORK

Distributed in the United States and Canada by St. Martin's Press

Pinter Publishers Ltd.
25 Floral Street, London WC2E 9DS, United Kingdom

First published in 1994

Distributed exclusively in the United States and Canada by St. Martin's Press, Inc., Room 400, 175 Fifth Avenue, New York, NY10010, USA

British Library Cataloguing in Publication Data

A CIP catalogue record for this book is available from the British Library

ISBN 1 85567 092 5 (hb)
ISBN 1 85567 093 3 (pb)

Library of Congress Cataloging in Publication Data

Attitudes to nature / edited by Jean Holm, with John Bowker.
p. cm. – (Themes in religious studies series)
Includes bibliographical references and index.
ISBN 1–85567–092–5. – ISBN 1–85567–093–3 (pbk.)
1. Nature – Religious aspects – Comparative studies. I. Holm, Jean, 1922– . II. Bowker, John Westerdale. III. Series.
BL435.A88 1994
291.2'4–dc20 94–15087
CIP

Typeset by Mayhew Typesetting, Rhayader, Powys
Printed and bound in Great Britain by Biddles Ltd., Guildford and King's Lynn

Contents

Series Preface

The person who knows only one religion does not know any religion. This rather startling claim was made in 1873, by Friedrich Max Müller, in his book, *Introduction to the Science of Religion.* He was applying to religion a saying of the poet Goethe: 'He who knows one language, knows none.'

In many ways this series illustrates Max Müller's claim. The diversity among the religious traditions represented in each of the volumes shows how mistaken are those people who assume that the pattern of belief and practice in their own religion is reflected equally in other religions. It is, of course, possible to do a cross-cultural study of the ways in which religions tackle particular issues, such as those which form the titles of the ten books in this series, but it soon becomes obvious that something which is central in one religion may be much less important in another. To take just three examples: the contrast between Islam's and Sikhism's attitudes to pilgrimage, in *Sacred Place*; the whole spectrum of positions on the authority of scriptures illustrated in *Sacred Writings*; and the problem which the titles, *Picturing God* and *Worship*, created for the contributor on Buddhism.

The series offers an introduction to the ways in which the themes are approached within eight religious traditions. Some of the themes relate particularly to the faith and practice of individuals and religious communities (*Picturing God, Worship, Rites of Passage, Sacred Writings, Myth and History, Sacred Place*); others have much wider implications, for society in general as well as for the religious communities themselves (*Attitudes to Nature, Making Moral Decisions, Human Nature and Destiny, Women in Religion*). This distinction, however, is not clear-cut. For instance, the 'sacred places' of Ayodhya and Jerusalem have figured in situations of national and international conflict, and some countries have passed laws regulating, or even banning, religious worship.

Stereotypes of the beliefs and practices of religions are so widespread that a real effort, of both study and imagination, is needed in order to discover what a religion looks – and feels – like to its adherents. We have to bracket out, temporarily, our own beliefs and presuppositions, and 'listen in' to a religion's account of what *it* regards as significant. This is not a straightforward task, and readers of the books in this series will encounter a number of the issues that characterise the study of religions, and that have to be taken into account in any serious attempt to get behind a factual description of a religion to an understanding of the real meaning of the words and actions for its adherents.

First, the problem of language. Islam's insistence that the Arabic of the Qur'ān cannot be 'translated' reflects the impossibility of finding in another language an exact equivalent of many of the most important terms in a religion. The very word, Islam, means something much more positive to a Muslim than is suggested in English by 'submission'. Similarly, it can be misleading to use 'incarnation' for *avatāra* in Hinduism, or 'suffering' for *dukkha* in Buddhism, or 'law' for Torah in Judaism, or 'gods' for *kami* in Shinto, or 'heaven' for *T'ien* in Taoism, or 'name' for *Nām* in Sikhism.

Next, the problem of defining – drawing a line round – a religion. Religions do not exist in a vacuum; they are influenced by the social and cultural context in which they are set. This can affect what they strenuously reject as well as what they may absorb into their pattern of belief and practice. And such influence is continuous, from a religion's origins (even though we may have no records from that period), through significant historical developments (which sometimes lead to the rise of new movements or sects), to its contemporary situation, especially when a religion is transplanted into a different region. For example, anyone who has studied Hinduism in India will be quite unprepared for the form of Hinduism they will meet in the island of Bali.

Even speaking of a 'religion' may be problematic. The term, 'Hinduism', for example, was invented by western scholars, and would not be recognised or understood by most 'Hindus'. A different example is provided by the religious situation in Japan, and the consequent debate among scholars as to whether they should speak of Japanese 'religion' or Japanese 'religions'.

Finally, it can be misleading to encounter only one aspect of a religion's teaching. The themes in this series are part of a whole interrelated network of beliefs and practices within each religious tradition, and need to be seen in this wider context. The reading lists at the end of each chapter point readers to general studies of the religions as well as to books which are helpful for further reading on the themes themselves.

Jean Holm
November 1993

List of Contributors

Jean Holm (EDITOR) was formerly Principal Lecturer in Religious Studies at Homerton College, Cambridge, teaching mainly Judaism and Hinduism. Her interests include relationships between religions; the relationship of culture to religion; and the way in which children are nurtured within a different cultural context. Her publications include *Teaching Religion in School* (OUP, 1975), *The Study of Religions* (Sheldon, 1977), *Growing up in Judaism* (Longman, 1990), *Growing up in Christianity*, with Romie Ridley (Longman, 1990) and *A Keyguide to Sources of Information on World Religions* (Mansell, 1991). She has edited three previous series: *Issues in Religious Studies*, with Peter Baelz (Sheldon), *Anselm Books*, with Peter Baelz (Lutterworth) and *Growing up in a Religion* (Longman).

John Bowker (EDITOR) was Professor of Religious Studies in Lancaster University, before returning to Cambridge to become Dean and Fellow of Trinity College. He is at present Professor of Divinity at Gresham College in London, and Adjunct Professor at the University of Pennsylvania and at the State University of North Carolina. He is particularly interested in anthropological and sociological approaches to the study of religions. He has done a number of programmes for the BBC, including the *Worlds of Faith* series, and a series on Islam and Hinduism for the World Service. He is the author of many books in the field of Religious Studies, including *The Meanings of Death* (Cambridge University Press, 1991), which was awarded the biennial Harper Collins religious book prize in 1993, in the academic section.

Douglas Davies is Professor of Religious Studies in the Department of Theology at the University of Nottingham, where he specialises in teaching the social anthropology of religion. He trained both in theology and social anthropology and his research continues to relate to both disciplines. His interest in theoretical and historical aspects of religious studies is represented in a major study of the sociology of knowledge and religion, published as *Meaning and Salvation in Religious Studies* (Brill, 1984), and in a historical volume, *Frank Byron Jevons 1858–1936, An Evolutionary Realist* (Edwin Mellen Press, 1991). Professor Davies is also very much concerned with practical aspects of religious behaviour and is a leading British scholar of Mormonism and, in addition to various articles, is author of *Mormon Spirituality* (Nottingham and Utah University Press, 1987). He was joint Director of the Rural Church Project, involving one of the largest sociological studies of religion in Britain published as *Church and Religion in Rural Britain* (with C. Watkins and M. Winter, T. & T. Clark, 1991). As Director of the Cremation Research Project he is conducting basic work on Cremation in Britain and Europe and has already produced some results in *Cremation Today and Tomorrow* (Grove Books, 1990).

Ian Harris is Senior Lecturer in Religious Studies at St Martin's College, Lancaster, with teaching responsibilities in the fields of Hindu and Buddhist thought. His research interests include contemporary Buddhism, the relationship between Indian medicine and Buddhist thought, and the impact of India on the West. Dr Harris' first book, *The Continuity of Madhyamaka and Yogacara in Early Buddhism* (E.J. Brill, 1991), details the overlap between two prominent Buddhist philosophical schools. He is also co-editor (with Stuart Mews, Paul Morris and John Shepherd) of *Contemporary Religions: A World Guide* (Longmans, 1992).

Anuradha Roma Choudhury is a Librarian working with the South Glamorgan County Library Service and is responsible for its Asian language section. She is also a part-time tutor with the Department of Continuing Education of University of Wales, Cardiff. She studied Sanskrit Literature at the University of Calcutta, India, and taught in schools for a number of years. She holds Gita-bharati diploma in Indian music from Calcutta and is an accomplished singer. She lectures extensively on topics related to Indian music, customs, family life and Hinduism. She is the author of a book on Indian music called *Bilati-gan-bhanga Rabindra-sangeet* (Influence of British music on Rabindranath Tagore's songs) written in Bengali and published in Calcutta, 1987. She is also one of the contributors to *The Essential Teachings of Hinduism* (ed. Kerry Brown, Rider, 1988). She is actively involved with multi-cultural arts and inter-faith groups.

Martin Forward is Secretary of the Methodist Church's Committee for Relations with People of Other Faiths, and a Consultant to the Council of Churches for Britain and Ireland's Commission for Inter-Faith relations. He used to work in the Henry Martyn Institute for Islamic Studies, Hyderabad, India. Martin Forward has taught an introductory course on Islam at Leicester University, and now teaches courses on Islam at Bristol University.

Mohamed Alam grew up in Lahore, Pakistan, where he was a student at the University of the Panjab. He now lives in Leicester where he is President of the Rawal Community, an organisation of Panjābi Muslims. He teaches Urdu at a school in Peterborough.

Norman Solomon is founder and Director of the Centre for the Study of Judaism and Jewish/Christian Relations at the Selly Oak Colleges, Birmingham. He is Visiting Lecturer to the Oxford Centre for Postgraduate Hebrew Studies, adviser to the International Council of Christians and Jews, and Vice Chairman of the World Congress of Faith. Among his many publications is *Judaism and World Religion* (Macmillan, 1991). Rabbi Dr Solomon has a particular interest in Christian Jewish dialogue and has been a frequent participant in international dialogue events with the World Council of Churches, the Vatican and the Ecumenical Patriarchate. He is also involved in trilateral dialogues of Jews, Christians and Muslims.

Kanwaljit Kaur-Singh is a local authority inspector for primary education. Her research interests concern the contribution of women to Sikh society. She has spoken extensively on issues relating to Sikh religion and primary education, and has written articles on education and racial equality. Dr Kaur-Singh is currently Chair of the British Sikh Education Council.

Xinzhong Yao is Lecturer in Chinese religion and ethics at the

University of Wales, Lampeter. His research interests include philosophy, ethics and religion; he is currently focusing on comparative philosophy and comparative religion. Dr Yao is author of *On Moral Activity* (People's University Press, Beijing, 1990), *Ethics and Social Problems* (City Economic Press, Beijing, 1989), co-author of *Comparative Studies on Human Nature* (Tienjin People's Press, Tienjin, 1988) and co-editor of *Applying Ethics* (Jilin People's Press, Changchun, 1994), and main translator of Charles L. Stevenson's *Ethics and Language* (Social Sciences of China Press, Beijing, 1991). He is a member of the Chinese National Association of Ethics and Deputy Director of the Institute of Ethics, the People's University of China. Beijing.

Brian Bocking is Professor and Head of the Department of Study of Religions, Bath College of Higher Education. He formerly lectured on Japanese religions at the University of Stirling and has spent a year lecturing at the University of Tsukuba, Japan. His main teaching and research interests include Japanese religions, Chinese and Japanese Buddhism, mysticism and comparative religion. Professor Bocking is author of 'Reflections on Soka Gakkai' in *The Scottish Journal of Religious Studies* (1981), 'Comparative Studies of Buddhism and Christianity' in *Japanese Journal of Religious Studies* (1983), 'The Japanese Religious Traditions in Today's World' in *Religion and Today's World* (ed. F. Whaling; T&T Clark, Edinburgh, 1987), 'Factionalism in Japanese Religion' in *Japan Forum* (1989), and 'The Origins of Japanese Philosophy' in *The Encyclopaedia of Asian Philosophy* (eds Carr and Mahalingham, Routledge, forthcoming).

Introduction: Raising the Issues

Douglas Davies

Perhaps fish are quite unaware of water. Being so much part of their world they cannot, as it were, stand back and rationalise about it. Perhaps *nature* is rather similar for people in many cultures. It is so much a part and parcel of their lives that they do not try to stand back and analyse it. This is an especially important point to bear in mind for this book, keeping us alert to see how some religions immerse themselves in nature while others draw back from it.

As others see nature

In religious studies it is always important to try and see the world as other people see it without, unthinkingly, imposing our own perspective on others. There are several complementary methods used in religious studies to help in the task of gaining insight into the religious outlook, beliefs and practices of others, and these are drawn upon in this introduction to help readers approach each subsequent chapter.

Methods of approach

The history of religions shows how religious ideas and practices have developed over long periods of time, and this is particularly useful as far as attitudes to nature are concerned. It is only in the later part of the twentieth century that western societies have focused on nature as part of a scientific and economic concern about ecology. Most religions have been concerned with nature for thousands of years in the sense that they have doctrines of creation, but only in modern times has there emerged a self-conscious and explicit concern over nature itself. It is one thing to have a doctrine of creation and quite another to become actively concerned about the world.

Some might argue that the modern world's growing moral concern to preserve endangered species or to protect the ozone layer is not a religious issue at all but a kind of secularised value, a concern for the planet as the environment of our species. This is an interesting and debatable point and could mean that the world itself, rather than its creator, has come to be the focus of concern. These are all problems which can be studied in a historical way.

Another approach comes from the phenomenology of religion, which tries to identify and describe religious experience and ideas making up the religious life of people. By understanding our own religious or philosophical outlook we strive to put them aside for a moment while we look at the religious experience of others. Instead of always trying to compare and contrast our view of nature with that of someone else, we simply try to see how they look at themselves and the world. Each of the following chapters presents the attitude to nature of a major religious culture in such a way that readers can begin to see how others feel and think about the world in which they live. In the chapter on Chinese religions, for example, we see how ritual – *li* – is a means of integrating the life of earth and the heavens as part of the grand order of things.

Yet another form of study is that of the anthropology of religion which studies the way different societies live in the here and now, trying to find the pattern of values underlying the innumerable beliefs and practices of daily life. One idea drawn from anthropology – that of cultural classification – is particularly important for this book. 'Classification' is a term used to describe the way a society organises its world. So, for example, the chapter on Japanese religions shows the whale classified as a fish and not as a mammal. This does not mean that the Japanese teach biology in a different way from western scientific biologists; in the shared world of science whales are defined as mammals, but in everyday life, as far as organising food is concerned, whales are treated 'like' fish and not 'like' cows.

From bias to perspective

Each society has its own way of organising the world, and our own perspectives are so ingrained in us that we normally take them completely for granted. Often this classification of reality has its roots in the ancient past but major changes can also take place. An example of such change is given in Chapter 2: Christianity, where the theory of evolution, propounded in the mid-nineteenth century and dramatically altering the way many people came to understand humanity, is discussed.

So, as far as this book is concerned, the way each religious culture classifies 'nature' is of paramount importance. Each chapter can be read not as though 'nature' is a definite and clear concept meaning the same thing in all parts of the world, but as a challenge to see just what 'nature' does mean within a particular religious tradition. This also suggests that, from the very outset, we do not assume that the idea of 'nature' will have the same history or significance in each religion.

Religions, themselves, are changing realities, responding to world circumstances and developing through their perception of ultimate reality. The impact of science and technology on the world has, for example, triggered a response in some religions – especially in Christianity as the dominant religion in western industrial and scientific societies, so that its attitude to nature has come to be on the theological agenda for the first time in its history.

Classifying nature

The remainder of this introduction briefly sketches the attitudes to nature reflected in the following chapters as a rapid exercise in the phenomenology of religion, focusing on the value given to the idea of nature within the religion as the basis of assessment. By 'value' we mean the degree to which nature is identified as a positive and vital part of the religious life or as a negative element with no ultimate part to play in the goal of religious existence.

This results in what we might call a classification of 'classification of nature' with three broad divisions: the givenness of nature, the created order of nature, and the potential illusion of nature. In Japanese and Chinese traditional religions the world is taken for granted as part of life in which people must come to a sense of balance. Then, in Judaism, Christianity and Islam, we see a strong doctrine of creation producing an objectively real world in which people are to live in obedience to and love of God. Finally, in Sikhism, Hinduism and Buddhism we find a natural world which is a potential illusion, open to trap the unwary into a materialism which prevents the freedom of spiritual insight.

It is important to remember that this scheme is only one of many possible ways of arranging these religions in their attitudes to nature. Other scholars may adopt a different approach to illustrate and draw out some other emphases.

Nature in religions

First we begin with Japanese religions, where nature is accepted as part of the givenness of the world as opposed to a self-conscious concern with ecology. The Confucian ethic stresses social harmony and the well-being of the community within its natural world. There is an optimism about the world itself, with no idea that the world will come to an end. As Bocking so clearly says, there is no world to be saved from and there is no need for the world to be saved from us. He stresses that the idea of a global disaster is an essentially western concept, a pessimism quite contrary to the intrinsic optimism of Japanese religions.

The chapter on Chinese religions takes up a similar need for harmony between people and their environment as expressed, for example, in the paired ideas of *yin* and *yang*. Together this pair help compose a system of classification embracing many sorts of things. Then the idea of *tao* expresses the universal principle of order and is related to the virtue, power, or *te* with which *tao* endows everyone. Humanity and nature are all part of the same scheme of things. To fulfil one's *te* is to be natural as one absorbs the essence of the universe.

Though it might seem natural to discuss Buddhist thought next this will not be done because it is not intrinsically optimistic about nature, as will soon become apparent.

Judaism is a very clear example of a system of classification of nature through its creation myths, where everything is organised into a hierarchical scheme of created things. Even the highly-structured way Solomon writes the chapter reflects an order and organisation which is also believed to exist in nature. As he says in his 'Model Jewish Statement on Nature', creation is good and reflects the glory of its creator, and precisely because of this it should not be wasted in any way. This chapter also shows how religious ideas from the past can be drawn upon anew to deal with novel problems such as global warming and nuclear energy. Here the adaptability of a religious system of thought becomes very clear.

Christianity shows its historical links with Judaism in giving a very positive value to the world of nature, which has been created by God as a very real environment. But within Christianity it is obvious that a variety of moral values have been used to interpret this world of matter. On the one hand it is a real but 'fallen' world, which needs transforming by God at some future time, but on the other it is also seen as already having been given a particular stamp of divine approval in the belief that God has actually shared in the material nature of the world through the life of Jesus of Nazareth. The chapter on Christianity reflects this 'introduction' in showing how the word 'nature' can have different meanings, and also shows how historical developments, such as the theory of evolution, can influence theological thought in fundamental ways. But not all Christians place a high value on nature; some see it as such a fallen world that they long to be in heaven as their new environment.

Islam reflects something of this view in not giving an eternal value to nature, but seeing it as humanity's temporary home prior to the resurrection and the ultimate goal of paradise. The whole of the universe is deemed to be under the law of God and, in that sense, the creation follows Islam and everything is *muslim*, for all is in submission to the will of God. 'Nature' is a very broad concept and is not simply restricted to animals and plants; angels and *jinn* are also part of creation in a world that reaches beyond the senses. The chapter on Islam also argues that, whether in the environment of the desert or of cities, Muslims have, for example, sought an equilibrium with the natural world through their pattern of housing, whether in tents or fixed architecture. One clear example of Islamic classification of the world is the distinction between *ḥalāl* (permissible) and *ḥarām* (harmful) foods. Even the killing of animals for food is defined as a devotional act, something that reflects the case in Judaism but which is quite different from the slaughter of animals in more traditionally Christian cultural contexts where it is a practical and utilitarian act.

In the case of Sikh culture we move to a world view in which nature expresses the creativity of God, is capable of prompting humankind into an awareness of the divine, but which is also a potential trap for sensuous living. Above all else, this arena of the world is a prompt for the spiritual life and an aid for devotion. One interesting example of a form of classification comes in the link between the universe as the macrocosm and the body as a microcosm, each reflecting the other. Like the body, the visible universe is also transitory and will come to its end. But while life exists it is possible for men and women to attain to salvation, to see through the illusory nature of apparent reality, and live a life of service to others. The world, despite its negative features which can lead people into increasing selfishness and illusion, is still the arena in which people can live with one thought dwelling on the true God and another firmly fixed on practical concerns.

Relationship with the world of nature lies at the heart of Hinduism. The earliest literature, the *Ṛg-veda*, not only shows a reverence for such natural phenomena as sun, wind, rain and storms, but includes speculation about the mystery of creation, a speculation which was developed over the centuries in a series of creation myths. Alongside this 'wider perspective of the creation as a whole', Choudhury sets the 'intimate perspective of the Mother Earth', with humans recognising a kinship with the whole of nature – animate and inanimate.

It is only now at the end of this series of attitudes to nature that Buddhism can be considered, with its matured negative view of the material world of nature. According to Buddhist thought all things share in impermanence so that, for example, as Harris mentions in his chapter, issues like the preservation of the black rhinoceros take on a particular significance since they too will ultimately pass away like all other things. Here, purpose and meaning are not an integral part of any created universe. Harris shows how the Buddhist ethic, as far as animals are concerned, is instrumental and serves the goals of spirituality. The Buddha's teaching, he says, views the world in a sombre light, with little opportunity for nature mysticism. There is no supreme creator because the major emphasis is upon the mental and spiritual development of each Buddhist. Consciousness assumes priority over nature. Nature has to be classified aright, not in the sense of its being a hierarchical order of created things but as a world which no longer entraps the sensuous individual.

Style and nature

We have now seen that 'nature' has several different meanings across world religions, and in the following chapters we have an opportunity to see how each author chooses to dwell now on one feature and now on another. The style of each chapter does, up to a point, express something about that religion's own attitude to nature.

1. Buddhism

Ian Harris

Ecological thinking has come to the fore in the late twentieth century. If this view is accepted, then one will be hard pressed to discover more than the odd resonance of environmentalism in the literature of the ancient world. This fact is recognised by many influential representatives of the ecological movement today. Thus, Eugene C. Hargrove (1989), in his examination of the thought of ancient Greece, concludes that it was impossible for Greek philosophy to think ecologically. The metaphysical assumptions underpinning much of the thought current at that time were clearly at variance with those operating today; therefore a concern for the natural world is highly problematic in the Greek context.

It may seem rather strange to begin a discussion on the attitude of Buddhism to the environment by reference to Greek thought, but there is method in my madness. In an influential and, in terms of recent interest in environmental ethics, early piece of work, John Passmore (1980) concludes that western philosophy is incompatible with a concern for nature. Passmore is particularly scornful of the negative role played by Christianity. For him the doctrine of human dominion over nature, found in the writings of Augustine, Aquinas, Calvin, etc., has done much to alienate the modern industrialised world from its natural environment. More recent commentators on the impact of Christianity on environmental ethics have shown that Passmore tends to overstate his case. Robin Attfield (1983) is a good case in point. While it is true that some remarkably negative statements on our relations with nature are to be found in the writings of major theologians, another more positive tradition of stewardship and care for the environment runs side by side with the negative throughout most of the history of Christianity. This attitude is exemplified in the traditions of Francis of Assisi, and in the works of some Orthodox theologians. Christianity, then, appears to contain an essentially negative official attitude to the environment, underpinned by an influential but minority position far more favourable to an environmentalist ethic. Some writers, most notably Lynn White Jnr (1967), have claimed that eastern religions, and Buddhism in particular, are more explicitly positive in their concern for the natural world. I find this attitude difficult to square with any actually occurring Buddhist tradition and shall argue that the Christian situation is more or less precisely mirrored in Buddhism.

Buddhism and the natural world

In its earliest phases Buddhism was essentially a world-denying religion. Existence was conceived of as having the characteristics of suffering (*dukkha*), impermanence (*anicca*) and insubstantiality (*anattā*) and thus the goal of the monk (i.e. *nirvāṇa*) was thought of as outside this world. In other words, the best thing that one could do was to turn one's back on the world – to escape from it. The essence of this way of thinking is contained in the Buddha's celebrated first sermon in which he outlines the Four Noble Truths. In this sermon we hear of the inherent unsatisfactoriness of conditioned things (i.e. the idea that all causally produced entities are impermanent and, as such, fail to confer happiness), and of the path which leads away from the suffering associated with the world. It is not surprising, given this rather sombre vision, that the early Buddhist texts fail, in any systematic way, to develop a coherent world picture. Beyond the occasional snippet of information, the Pāli canon of Theravāda Buddhism, the earliest collection of Buddhist scriptures available, is notable in its lack of cosmological lore. It seems, almost studiously, to avoid any discussion of cosmic and human origins. This is probably connected to the character of early Buddhism which denies the existence of one divine creator, though Buddhists have always accepted the existence of a plurality of gods who have the capacity to bring about real effects in the human realm. The recognition and appeasement of these divine beings is enormously important in the lives of rural lay Buddhists today, but, having said this, it is clear that Buddhism is unique in the religions of the world for its disinclination to offer a prominent theory of creation. It is difficult to know precisely why, but this situation was not allowed to continue in the Buddhist tradition down to the present day.

Approximately 1,000 years after the death of the Buddha a number of prominent Buddhist commentators appeared on the scene, and they seemed to recognise the need for a more fully worked out cosmology than that present in the canon itself. Perhaps this shift in position was felt to be necessary in order to get into effective dialogue with, and demonstrate superiority over, members of other religious traditions, most notably the Hindus. Certainly at this stage in their history the Hindus had a fairly complex and elegant world picture, which possessed the advantage that it could be used to predict certain simple natural phenomena, such as the distinction between night and day. One assumes that their Buddhist opponents may have felt at a bit of a disadvantage. In time, then, the Hindu world picture was adopted by the rival religious tradition and revised to bring it into line with fundamental Buddhist axioms. The two most prominent Buddhists in this connection are Vasubandhu, a fourth-century writer from northern India, and Buddhaghosa, a very exceptional commentator on the Pāli canon, who lived approximately a century after Vasubandhu. This being the case, the relatively late *Abhidharmakośa* of Vasubandhu, and the *Visuddhimagga* of Buddhaghosa, provide us with the most comprehensive descriptions of the world as seen from a Buddhist point of view. They are remarkably consistent with each other and I shall draw on both for the following description.

In line with Hindu thought, Buddhists hold that the world is periodically brought into being and, at a later stage, many millions of years in the future, it is destroyed. This process has no beginning and no end. In this sense, the Indian religions differ from Judaism, Christianity and Islam. Unlike the latter traditions, which hold an essentially linear idea of history based on a definite starting point and an equally definite conclusion to the world process, Indian thought prefers to deal in enormously long cycles of history, one following the other for all eternity. In other words, the cosmos persists for a lengthy period, is dissolved, and at some stage in the future is again brought forth out of the void until it meets the same fate, and so on, and on. Now this fact alone provides us with a useful means by which we may contrast the Buddhist understanding of existence with that more familiar to us from the Christian tradition, in which creation is brought into being by a benign and purposeful creator.

The purpose or meaning of the Buddhist world order is more difficult to establish. For one thing it does not come into being as the result of the activities of a Supreme Being. In the second place, there is no indication that it is moving towards any condition of fulfilment. It simply runs on, from one cycle to another, *ad infinitum*. Rather than being a purposeful process leading inevitably to an unknown but meaningful conclusion, the Buddhist vision of the world is more pessimistic. The world is endless, meaningless and purposeless. This does not mean that the Buddhist must be seized by despair, for after all the Buddha has taught the means to escape from conditioned existence. As such, the Buddha's teaching (*dharma*) is regarded as a very remarkable thing, the greatest of all gifts. Nevertheless, the world is viewed, particularly in the earliest phase of Buddhism, as a vicious circle (*saṃsāra*). Knowledge that this is so leads to the inevitable desire to find the means of escape from such an unsatisfactory state. Since desires for worldly things are considered to bind us even more strongly to existence and increase our suffering, Buddhism extols the virtues of the world-renouncer. For Buddhism, the renouncer *par excellence* is the monk (*bhikkhu*). Membership of the monastic community (*saṅgha*) is considered to be the most effective means of hastening one's spiritual liberation.

The traditions preserved in the Pāli canon give the strong impression that during the Buddha's lifetime a considerable number of persons experienced liberation. On the attainment of enlightenment (*nirvāṇa*), a person is referred to as an *arhat*. Study of the relevant early texts seems to suggest that arhatship could be brought about in two basic ways. For some individuals, presumably already far advanced on the path as a result of their own efforts, merely hearing the word of the Buddha was sufficient. However, the majority of *arhat*s were required to put the teachings they received from the Buddha into practice for some finite period in order to achieve *nirvāṇa*. In effect, the methods recommended in the teachings fairly rapidly brought the practitioner to a state in which all desires were uprooted. Now it seems as though the death of the Buddha brought these spectacular and sudden transformations in spiritual status pretty much to an end.

As time went on, the time required for a monk to achieve

liberation increased. The canon tells us that the Buddha predicted such a state of affairs. He taught that, from the time of his death, the teachings (*dharma*) would go slowly and inexorably into decline until the stage was reached when they would disappear altogether. Perhaps the increased time that a monk appears to have needed in order to attain his goal was a function of this decline in the *dharma*. Another explanation is simply that the fervour of the early period, in which the founder was still present and ministering to his disciples, was replaced by a more relaxed attitude to the possibility of liberation. Whatever the explanation, a new attitude towards the world and the beings it contains began to develop. The spiritual path began to take on a more gradual character. The possibility of sudden enlightenment began to seem less realistic. As a result, the likelihood of a monastic career spanning a good many lives (perhaps many millions of lives) became the norm. In this way the career of the monk began to share some of the characteristics of the lay path, which had been seen as an enormously lengthy process from the earliest period of Buddhist history. Not surprisingly, the radical other-worldliness of the early period is pushed out of the foreground in the thinking of the *saṅgha*, and a slightly more positive vision of the world begins to form. It should be noted that the Buddhist laity probably always regarded the natural world in a more concerned manner than the largely urban members of the *saṅgha*. It is a pity that we do not possess any substantial account of their views on the subject, though this is not surprising, given the fact that learning and literacy were almost entirely the preserve of the monks. Nevertheless, as the tradition develops and becomes more realistic, even the outlook of its community of renouncers starts to see the natural world in a new light.

The description of the world contained in the writings of Vasubandhu and Buddhaghosa has come down to the Buddhists of the present day virtually unchanged. In this respect Buddhism differs from Christianity. In the Christian tradition a radical redrawing of the cosmos was occasioned by the crisis caused by the rise of science in the early modern period. The findings of Galileo and Copernicus, despite initial condemnation by the church, were ultimately to win the day. However, the essentially alien nature of western scientific thinking has had a marginal impact on the traditional systems of thought of Asia, perhaps because, at least in part, the status of myth and story has been higher in the East than in the West (cf. Bowker,

1990). Nevertheless, recent evidence suggests that in some regions of the Buddhist world, most notably in Thailand and Sri Lanka, the situation is changing, and Buddhist doctrine is, in educated circles, coming to align itself with the findings of science.

For traditional Buddhism the world in which we live is a golden disk floating on a mighty cosmic ocean. This ocean is in turn supported by a circle of wind which itself rests on space. In one of the few cosmological fragments of the Pāli canon, the Buddha explains that earthquakes may be caused by turbulence in the circle of wind which causes a similar effect in the ocean. This is communicated to the golden earth which then shakes. Many contemporary Buddhists, particularly in Sri Lanka, regard this as a surprisingly modern view of the origin of earthquakes, but when read in context, we discover that this is only one special category of earthquake discussed in the text. By far the most prominent of the explanations given for these apparently natural occurrences is based on non-naturalistic principles. Most earthquakes are ascribed to the activities of a *buddha*. Decisive moments in the life of one destined to obtain enlightenment, such as his birth, renouncing of home, moment of enlightenment, death, etc., are said to be accompanied by earthquakes.

An enormous mountain, Mount Meru, some 84,000 *yojana*s high (one *yojana* = c. nine miles) is said to be situated at the centre of our golden earth. It is surrounded by seven concentric rings of mountains, each one half the height of the former as one moves outwards to the perimeter of the disc. All of the mountains are golden. At the extreme rim of the disc is a circle of iron mountains. Between the last range of golden mountains and circles of iron (*cakravāla*) we find an ocean. Four island continents are located at the four cardinal points within this ocean. Humans live on the most southerly of the islands, which, because of the nature of its vegetation, is called the Rose-Apple land (*Jambudvīpa*). We are said to share this land with the animals and the hungry ghosts (*preta*s). Animals also flourish in the ocean surrounding our continent. On terraces cut into the slopes of Mount Meru live the gods (*deva*s), their status in the divine hierarchy determined by their position on the mountain. At the summit is the palace of Indra, the chief deity in vedic times. Other gods with more subtle bodies are held to exist in realms above the summit. At a distance as far below the earth as Indra's palace is above it, we find the abodes of the denizens of hell.

There are a range of hellish existences, each one characterised by a different form of suffering for its inhabitants. In the Buddhist cosmos, then, five distinct kinds of being are to be found, i.e. humans, animals, ghosts, gods and denizens of hell. Some texts add a sixth group, the demi-gods (*asura*s), who spend their time locked in conflict with the gods themselves.

These six discrete destinies (*gati*) are interrelated. As beings eternally process around the circle of birth and deaths (*saṃsāra*) they are destined to spend innumerable lives in each of the *gati*s. As a consequence, we are intimately related to a very wide range of beings. A horse in the field may, for instance, have been our brother in a previous existence. This state of affairs clearly leads to a strong feeling of solidarity and fellow feeling with all beings. We are all in the same boat together. We are all circulating through various forms of suffering (even the divine destinies involve suffering, though on a more subtle level than we experience as humans), and are all, in our own way, destined to obtain eventual release.

A visually striking representation of the six destinies is found in the Buddhist wheel of life (*bhavacakra*). These complex and symbolic works of art are found particularly in the Tibetan tradition, and consist of a six-spoked wheel in which the gaps between the spokes contain scenes depicting the life-styles of beings in each of the six *gati*s. At the hub of the wheel one generally finds three animals in a circle attempting to devour the tail of the creature in front. These are the pig, the cockerel and the snake, which respectively represent greed, hatred and delusion, the three aspects of ignorance (*avidyā*) which is the destructive principle at the root of all forms of existence. The message of this image is straightforward. No perfection is possible within the realm of conditioned things. Everything, no matter how attractive it appears on the surface, is marked by suffering (*dukkha*), impermanence (*anicca*) and insubstantiality (*anattā*). Without going into enormous detail, it might be worth examining one further feature of the wheel of life (*bhavacakra*). The outer rim of the wheel contains a series of twelve images which, when put together, depict the progress of beings from one life to another. The strength of the series is that it explains the inevitability of the causal process at work in the world. Our desires are shown to bind us ever more closely to the world, with the consequence that on death the force of our desire impels us on into a new life. This life, even if it reaches its natural span, must inevitably close with old age, sickness and death. Yet still our desires force us ever onward into fresh forms of existence. The principle of causation which imparts the sense of inevitability to things was the fundamental discovery of the Buddha on attaining enlightenment. It is referred to as dependent origination (*pratītyasamutpāda*) and the series of twelve images on the rim of the wheel represent an attempt to give this principle visual form.

Some recent scholars have claimed that the Sanskrit word *pratītyasamutpāda* is the nearest equivalent in Buddhist sources to our term 'nature'. They go on to argue that since this is so, it is self-evidently the case that Buddhism, from its inception, has had a concern for nature. We now need to examine this view in more depth. The doctrine of dependent origination (*pratītyasamutpāda*) highlights the Buddhist notion that all apparently substantial entities within the world are in fact wrongly perceived. We live under the illusion that terms such as 'I', self, mountain, tree, etc., denote permanent and stable things. The doctrine teaches that this is not so. What appears to be permanent is, in fact, in a state of perpetual flux. The Theravadin position is that the ordinary objects of consciousness may actually be resolved into a stream of momentary and mutually conditioning entities called *dharma*s. Someone skilled in meditation may observe the rise and fall of these *dharma*s. For them the illusion of permanence and substantiality is undermined at a more fundamental level by the flux of radical change. The world is like a raging torrent which never remains the same from one moment to the next. Now, modern environmentalist thinking makes much of the interdependence of things in the natural world, and it is certainly true that the doctrine of *pratītyasamutpāda* is in tune with a world view which accepts complex, interdependent relationships. However, there is a problem associated with making a comparison between Buddhism and environmentalist thinking which the scholars mentioned above fail to acknowledge. The Buddhist analysis of things, be they animate or inanimate, is far more radical than that adopted by western ecology.

Let us take the example of an endangered species such as the black rhino. For the environmentalist the potential demise of these noble creatures is a matter of sadness and concern. To counteract this possibility, measures will be taken to protect the species by mitigating the destructive forces at work in the rhino's habitat, be they human-made or essentially independent of humanity. In this sense, environmentalism represents a 'fight against pollution and resource depletion'. A Buddhist is unlikely to view things in this way. I am not suggesting for one moment that Buddhists would rejoice at the extinction of the black rhino – very far from it – but, as we have previously noted, change, dissolution, suffering and death are the hallmarks of all conditioned things. At the deepest level, what we take to be a rhino is nothing more than a complex series of momentary *dharma*s which have come together in a certain pattern. To the eye of ignorance this patterning appears as a bulky, African quadruped. Looked at from a different perspective, the rise and fall of things, whether they be mountains or animals is part of the inexorable process Buddhists call *saṃsāra*. In a sense, contemplation of this fact brings home to us our own lack of substance and permanence. It may have a positive impact on the development of the spiritual life. The recognition of this deep impermanence may prompt us to investigate the teachings of the Buddha and opt to follow the Buddhist path which leads to *nirvāṇa*.

If we take stock of the argument to this point, it becomes clear that Buddhism does not provide the kind of doctrinal foundation from which environmental concerns can be easily developed in the way that some other religions, notably the semitic religions of Judaism, Christianity and Islam, do. In these traditions the natural world is the creation of a loving and Supreme Being. The natural world, since it is part of the created order, must have a distinct purpose in the divine scheme of things, and it can be coherently argued that humans must get their relations with this order right for the final purpose of existence to be realised. As we have already noted, Buddhism repudiates that kind of theism and the theistic response to the world. Purpose and meaning as such are missing from the equation, but we should be on our guard against misinterpreting the Buddhist outlook on the world. Far from being cold-hearted or nihilistic, Buddhism places great stress on loving-kindness and compassion to all beings. After all, we are all in the same boat. Let us now examine this strand of the tradition in more detail.

Non-injury in the Buddhist tradition

The principle of non-injury is one of the characteristic features of many ancient Indian religious traditions. There is some evidence to suggest that the avoidance of harming living things pre-dates the arrival of the Aryans in the subcontinent some 4,500 years ago. The religion of the Aryans, preserved as it is in the vedic writings, is an essentially sacrificial religion and, as such, was dependent from time to time on the sacrifice of animals. In contrast, we find no evidence of such practices in the classical system of Yoga or in the religion of the Jainas. The same may be said for Buddhism. It is noteworthy that these three traditions were essentially traditions of renunciants. Since renunciation is not easily reconciled with the martial and life-affirming world view of the Aryans, there may be some substance to the view that both renunciation and the practice of non-injury were indigenous Indian modes of behaviour. Certainly non-injury (*ahiṃsā*) is stressed quite frequently in the early texts of Buddhism.

The frequency of occurrence of this doctrine is at least partly explained by Buddhist adherence to the idea of rebirth. As we have already noted, our very large number of previous lives means that we have already established intimate relations with virtually the whole of the animal kingdom. We are in some, unconscious, sense part of an enormous family of fellow sufferers. To contribute to the further suffering of any individual member of this family would be as serious an offence as harming one's mother or father. Anthropologists and psychoanalysts tell us that offences of this kind are treated with particular opprobrium in the majority of cultures. However, in the Buddhist context the emphasis on non-harming may have another dimension. A number of texts teach that this practice may lead to a favourable future birth. The implication is clearly that harming results in rebirth in an unfavourable destiny (*gati*). Perhaps someone who has committed acts of cruelty to animals will become an animal, ghost or even a denizen of hell. In this sense, an act of cruelty contaminates the person who commits the deed – as a result he or she becomes impure. This impurity is viewed as a physical contaminant which drags the person down to a lower level of existence after death. If this interpretation is accepted, then there is something to be said for the view that non-injury (*ahiṃsā*) was regarded in a positive light as much for its purificatory role in a person's spiritual development as it was for its effects on animal and human welfare.

The case of vegetarianism brings this contrast to prominence. It is often assumed that the Buddha taught vegetarianism. This certainly seems to follow logically from the doctrine of non-injury. In fact, examination of the relevant sources reveals a rather more complicated situation. The Pāli canon reveals that the Buddha was himself occasionally to be found eating meat. Not only that, but, under certain conditions, he gave members of the *saṅgha* permission to eat meat. The only requirement for a monk is that the meat should be properly cooked and pure. In other words, the monk should neither see, hear nor suspect that the meat has been prepared specifically for him. A final proviso is that the monk should refrain from eating ten kinds of meat, e.g., the flesh of the snake, lion, elephant, dog, etc. It has been convincingly argued, by Ruegg (1980) and others, that strict vegetarianism only became a coherent position in Mahāyāna Buddhism, at a pretty late stage in the history of the tradition. We should bear two factors in mind here. In the first place, vegetarianism is not a necessary condition for concern for the environment. In the second, compassion for the fate of individual members of the animal kingdom is not the same as the more general concern for the destiny of species characteristic of much environmentalist literature.

In order to expand on the foregoing discussion, let us now turn to an aspect of Buddhist meditational practice. This is the cultivation of lovingkindness (*mettā*). A frequently recommended series of meditational subjects are the four divine abidings (*bramavihāra*s). Concentration on the *bramavihāra*s (i.e., loving kindness, *mettā*; compassion, *karuṇā*; sympathetic joy, *muditā*; and equanimity, *upekkhā*) is believed to form an important preliminary in the Buddhist system of mental cultivation. Of the four, the meditation on lovingkindness is perhaps the most widely practised. By extending *mettā* towards others, goodwill is promoted and the heart becomes filled with love. However, in a discussion of this practice in his influential work on meditation, called the Path of Purification (*Visuddhimagga*), Buddhaghosa mentions eleven advantages which accrue to the practitioners themselves. Strangely, no advantages are listed for the recipient of the *mettā*. At another point in the discussion, we are told to avoid the directing of *mettā* towards animals. It is thought to be better, certainly in the early stages of the practice, to confine one's attention to a human object, and preferably a human towards whom one harbours no strong feelings, whether they be positive or negative.

In the Pāli texts, the Buddha is occasionally described as extending *mettā* towards animals. However, when the context of these occurrences is examined, it is clear that the Buddha does this for a very specific purpose. It is done to calm an enraged animal. A good example of this is the occasion when an attempt was made on the Buddha's life. A mad elephant is set loose to trample him and his entourage, but, through the Buddha's defensive use of *mettā*, this dangerous situation is diffused. Clearly *mettā* practice is an important feature of the Buddhist path, but when we look into its rationale we are forced to draw surprising conclusions. In general, the advantages of the practice are felt by the practitioner not by the living being to whom it is directed. In particular, successful practice is believed to result in rebirth in one of the divine realms. Non-human focuses of *mettā* are only infrequently met with in the scriptures, and even when they are, the objective of the practitioner is to render a potential threat harmless. A good example of this is to be found in the chanting of a portion of one of the Buddha's sermons (A.ii.72 *Khandha Paritta*) as a charm to ward off dangerous snakes.

I have argued (Harris, 1991) that, when seen in this light, the Buddhist attitude towards animals is essentially instrumental. Its essential function is to aid the practitioner in his search for spiritual perfection, and any good done to the being to whom *mettā* is extended is merely a happy side-effect. This fact is actually recognised by the tradition itself, for the scriptures accept that the cultivation of the *brahmavihāra*s does not lead directly to *nirvāṇa*. Since the practice is directed towards beings within the world, the results are held to be basically mundane (*lokiya*). In effect, the attitudes of mind reflected by the practice express our highest ethical ideals, and these ideals can be applied only within the realm of conditioned things. It is important to emphasise the fact that these ideals in themselves do not bring about any supramundane achievement. They are not essentially Buddhist ideals. They simply refer to actions which are viewed in a positive light by society as a whole. Actually the scriptures acknowledge that *brahmavihāra* practice does not originate within the Buddhist tradition. It was employed by the sages of old and merely preserved by the Buddha. The Buddha was quite prepared to accept these ideals, particularly since they perform a clear role in the maintenance of civilised values, but he stressed that one must accept their fundamentally provisional nature. Ultimately they bind us more tightly to the world, when the goal must be release.

In view of what has been said above, it seems clear that kindness and the avoidance of cruelty are civilised forms of behaviour endorsed by the Buddhist tradition. In accordance with this principle, the Buddha recommended that his lay followers should take the welfare of their domestic animals seriously. For instance, cowherds are warned not to milk their herds dry. It is a common custom in Buddhist regions of South and Southeast Asia, even today, to release animals, and particularly birds, from captivity. This practice probably derives from the Buddha's command that monks should free animals caught in hunters' traps.

However, there is little doubt that, for Buddhism, animals belong some way down the hierarchy of beings. They occupy one of the three unfavourable destinies (*gati*s). They are less wise than humans and cannot make effective progress on the Buddhist path. They cannot, therefore, be admitted as members of the *saṅgha*, for their presence within the monastic community would be deleterious. In the literature of monastic discipline, the Buddha regularly lists animals alongside hermaphrodites, thieves, parent-killers and, most significantly, those guilty of the most heinous of all crimes, murderers of a *buddha*.

There are plenty of incidents within the canon in which animals behave impeccably, and in many respects better than the average human, but nevertheless the animal realm is in general something to be wary of. Animals are thought to be more vicious than humans. The forest-dwelling monk is particularly prone to the dangers represented by wild animals. He may be attacked by tigers or snakes. Hence the importance of the practice of *mettā* as a protective mechanism. Looked at from another perspective, he is subject to the depredations of many small creatures. Their cumulative effect is to make his existence in the forest distinctly uncomfortable. Insects, rats and the like are continually attacking his limited range of possessions. Now, though this may be inconvenient on one level, the monk can turn this to his advantage. The activity of the animal kingdom is an example, on the grand scale, of the process of decay which affects all conditioned things. Meditation on this fact can develop a deeper understanding of the impermanence, insubstantiality and suffering associated with the world. As a result, the monk's desires for worldly things diminish. In fact, the perception of danger may itself be utilised on the spiritual quest. Fear is a particularly strong emotional state. Its strength and associated physical effects may become meditational objects. Investigation of fear in this manner may lead to important insights into the functioning of the mental processes, and this in turn may lead to greater insight into the *dharma*. Certainly this practice is recommended by some meditation teachers in Thailand today. It is said to have a powerful therapeutic value.

Before moving on, let us summarise the conclusions of this section. Kindness towards animals is encouraged by Buddhism. Such kindness is in accordance with worldly conventions. On this level the Buddha has no argument with the ethics of his day. However, Buddhism ultimately expects to transcend such considerations, for the tradition ideally represents an attempt to escape from the restrictions imposed on us by our position as beings within the world. Concern for the animal kingdom is compatible with Buddhism but does not arise naturally from its central insights into the nature of reality. It can happily be taken along as baggage on the path to perfection, but at some stage it must be abandoned. In actual fact, many of the practices which seem, at one level, to be targeted at the welfare of animals, have as their ultimate aim the spiritual development of the practitioner. The Buddhist ethic in this area is essentially instrumental.

The natural environment and Buddhism

If Max Weber was correct, and there is some evidence to suggest that he was, then it looks likely that Buddhism has its origins in the growing urban centres of northern India some 500 years before Christ. Tradition holds that the Buddha's favourite residing places were parks and pleasure groves which came into the possession of the early *Saṅgha* as gifts from wealthy lay followers. These were clearly convenient places for the reception of alms from surrounding residents, and from such suburban locations the Buddha was well poised to extend his influence. A life spent in the heart of the jungle would hardly have been as useful in this respect. The Pāli canon indicates that the laying out of such areas was thought to be a highly meritorious action, but it is important to note that these locations are essentially artificial. They are made by humans.

In the *Cakkavatisihānadasutta*, an early Pāli text, a description of the far future, in which conditions have improved greatly on the present, is given. At that time, humans can expect a life span of approximately 80,000 years. However, cities then will have grown to such an extent that the countryside will have all but disappeared. Surprisingly, the text gives no hint that this will be an undesirable state of affairs. On the contrary, the wilderness will have been tamed, and this is portrayed as a positive advance for humanity. The text might be interpreted as evidence for the great confidence felt by early Buddhists in the superiority of urban over rural culture.

It is an acknowledged fact that Buddhist sources are rather light on glowing descriptions of the natural world. One or two passages can be identified in which the author appears to be delighting in the glories of nature, but these are few and far between. There is a good reason for this. The doctrinal content of the Buddha's teaching paints the world in a rather sombre light. It is subject to corruption and intrinsically unsatisfactory. It is possible that one may be instantaneously struck with aesthetic pleasure on viewing a natural scene, but for the Buddhist this can never be more than a fleeting perception. There is no value attached to holding on to such experiences. In such a doctrinal environment it is difficult for natural mysticism to take a firm hold. This is clearly in great contrast to Christianity. For the latter tradition, the world can be read as a text revealing evidence of the divine creator's purpose. The perception of beauty can draw one closer to an appreciation of the author of such beauty. In short, nature reveals God. This is impossible with Buddhism. I do not mean by this that Buddhists themselves may not rejoice in the astonishing profusion of the natural world; there is no intentional dourness in Buddhism. But they cannot be led on from such reflections to any ultimate end. Delight in the world can too easily be a stage on the way towards increased desire for more such delights, and this must eventually lead to further suffering.

Buddhism shares many of the characteristics of the ancient traditions of Indian renunciation. So, despite its possible urban roots, the ideal of forest-dwelling had an impact on at least a proportion of the Buddha's followers. The forest is the antithesis of the cultivated and cultured environment of the town. It is the home of a variety of wild beasts and for this reason alone it induces fear. But there is another attendant problem associated with the forest – it may also be a haven for any number of malicious spirits. As such it is a place of ill-will and wickedness. It is an alien land. As a consequence, nuns are prevented from taking up abode here; they may be seduced by unwholesome influences. Some forests are referred to by name in the Pāli texts, and we are told that they were once cleared for cultivation but became reforested as a result of the ill-will of certain sages. Lack of cultivation, then, has a certain connection with negative emotions and outright wickedness. Cultivation on the other hand is equated with righteousness.

However, the forest can be employed as a meditational device. A number of prominent Buddhist writers recommend mindfulness of the forest as a means of gaining insight into impermanence. Buddhaghosa, for instance, extols the positive consequences of attention to falling leaves, and in the Mahāyāna the forest is sometimes seen as a metaphor for *saṃsāra* itself. It is not surprising, then, to find that Buddhist literature is full of natural imagery to describe the course of spiritual progress. For instance, one is said to move from a state in which the path is not cultivated to one in which it is. One sows the seeds of merit in the field of the Buddha. One takes the middle path to enlightenment. Paths which wander through uncharted territory must be avoided.

Buddhist scriptures contain rather little to indicate how the vegetable kingdom should be treated. However, a few snippets of information may be gleaned from a reading of the texts of monastic discipline. Monks must avoid damage to plant life. Incurring such damage is an offence which requires expiation on the part of the monk. This seems a clear-cut matter, but on closer investigation it appears that the texts are primarily concerned with damage to crops. If this is so, then one wonders about the intention underlying the rule. Is it wrong to damage any form of plant life, or is there an offence only when cultivated produce is concerned? It is difficult to give a precise answer, but we know that monks are prohibited from engaging in agricultural activity. This ruling presumably arose for a variety of reasons. In the first place, farming is a full-time occupation and leaves little spare time for the cultivation of the spiritual life. On the other hand, agricultural activities, such as ploughing, digging, etc., lead inevitably to the accidental death of soil organisms. Perhaps the avoidance of damage to crops is a simple extension of this principle. Monks will naturally damage crops in the harvesting process, therefore, they should avoid agriculture entirely. Now this is a fairly specific regulation, and some evidence exists to suggest a more wide-ranging ethic. The Buddha is certainly said to have avoided all damage to seed and plant life. This may be interpreted as an extension of the principle of non-injury (*ahiṃsā*) to the vegetable kingdom. However, while monastic conduct may be regulated along such lines, the life of the lay Buddhist must necessarily be less exacting.

The vast majority of Buddhist populations, at all phases of the history of the tradition, have been tied to the land as a matter of life and death. The laity must ensure that adequate foodstuffs are available for their families, but they have an added responsibility: they must provide alms for members of the *saṅgha*. Under such conditions monks would be ill-advised to demand unrealistic levels of behaviour among the ordinary people. There is a gulf, then, between the expectations imposed on monks and those thought appropriate for the laity. Monks must avoid all activities which result in harm to flora and fauna. Failure to observe these measures will lead to failure on the path to *nirvāṇa*. The laity, on the other hand, is compelled, by circumstance, to inflict a moderate level of harm on the natural environment. Agriculture cannot take place without some damage. However, the undesirable consequences of agricultural activity are diminished by lay alms-giving. By making regular offering of food to the *saṅgha*, the lay person is ensured rebirth in a favourable destiny (*gati*) after death. Weber refers to this less restrictive code practised by the Buddhist laity as an 'insufficiency ethic'. The term implies that lay activity, while it may be determined by certain moral criteria, is not sufficient in itself to bring about the ultimate goal of the tradition, i.e. *nirvāṇa*.

Before leaving this section, it is necessary for us to investigate the status of plants in the Buddhist scheme of things. They are certainly not conceived of as inanimate objects. They are thought to possess the single sense of touch, though none of the other faculties is present, e.g. the hearing, taste, mind, etc., which characterise higher organisms. They can nevertheless experience pain. It is apparent from our earlier discussion that the world of plants is not one of the six destinies – we can never be reborn as a tree or piece of grass. This is noteworthy because some Hindu *dharma* texts do accept this as a possibility. For Buddhism, though, the realm of vegetable life stands apart from the sphere of beings ultimately destined for enlightenment. It is part of the stage on which salvation is played, but does not itself possess the capacity for perfection. From the perspective of enlightenment, plant life shares in the purposelessness and meaninglessness of the entire realm of conditioned things. This does not mean that Buddhists may treat the vegetable kingdom with contempt. An individual's role as lay person or monk will be a crucial factor in determining the precise manner in which responsibilities are exercised, but the principle of non-injury must always be present as the background to behaviour. The major difference is that the *saṅgha* member works with a hard interpretation of the principle, while the lay person adopts a softer approach.

Conclusion

It is obvious that Buddhism starts with a very different set of priorities from those encountered in the religions of the ancient Near East. Its lack of a supreme creator, plus an insistence on the eternity of the world process, stand in stark contrast to the Judaeo-Christian tradition. In its origin Buddhism is a religion of world-weariness, though this situation clearly underwent significant modification as the centuries progressed. Nevertheless, the Buddha's prime importance as a religious teacher was his identification of the world as a domain devoid of substantiality. Recognition of this fact results in non-reliance on the things of the world. In consequence, the typical follower of the Buddha in the early period is a renouncer.

In essence and theory, then, Buddhism cannot uphold an environmentalist ethic. The reason for this is straightforward. There is nothing within the sphere of nature which can be said to possess any meaning or purpose. There can be no Buddhist justification for the fight to preserve habitats and environments. Everything, without exception, is subject to decay. It is not at all clear that change, within the natural world, can be positively affected by human interventions.

In practice, however, the situation is a little different. Since its inception Buddhism has been a missionary religion. In order to increase its influence in Asia, missionary monks have seen the sense in preserving local traditions as long as they do not come into conflict with central doctrinal concerns. The result of this activity has been that in many regions of the Buddhist world the renunciatory concerns of the early period have rested lightly on the lay population. We also know that the Buddha himself adopted an ethical outlook which drew substantially from pre-Buddhist systems of thought. From our perspective, his most important borrowing was the insistence on non-injury (*ahiṃsā*). Buddhists are expected to apply this principle in their dealings with all beings. All actions – be they bodily, verbal or mental – are to be referred back to this ideal. This is the essence of right action, one of the members of the noble eightfold path.

A consequence of this insistence is that animals and plants are to be respected and such respect arises naturally from the insight, provided by Buddhist cosmology, that all sentient beings are intimately interrelated. The level at which the principle of non-injury may be practised is effectively determined by a person's status in the Buddhist community. Agriculturalists must attempt to protect animal life but some injury is unavoidable, owing to the nature of the work. Monks are prevented from working on the land, for the negative consequences entailed by such tasks would be harmful to the spread of the *dharma*.

We should not imagine that the doctrine of *ahiṃsā* was imported into Buddhism without modification. On the contrary, it had to be incorporated into a coherent vision of things. The justification for non-injury is essentially instrumental. By behaving in a loving and compassionate fashion, one is ensured a favourable rebirth as a god (*deva*). This does not mean that the beings to whom love is directed will not benefit. In fact they will have their unfortunate lives enhanced, particularly if they are animals, and may in time come to a fuller understanding of the *dharma*.

In short, Buddhism endorses a spirit of toleration and co-operation with the natural world. It does so because this traditional mode of behaviour is given a specific sense by the tradition, and in the final analysis does not come into conflict with the ultimate goal, which is escape. From the perspective of enlightenment nothing may have a final purpose or essential value, but, at least in the early stages of the spiritual path, Buddhism acts as though it does. Here then is one of the many paradoxes encountered in the study of this unique religious system of thought.

FURTHER READING

Attfield, R. (1983) 'Western Traditions and Environmental Ethics', in Eliot, R. and Gane, A. (eds), *Environmental Philosophy*, Milton Keynes, Open University Press.

Bowker, J.W. (1990) 'Cosmology, Religion and Society', *Zygon*, 25: 7–23.

Hargrove, E.C. (1989) *Foundations of Environmental Ethics*, Englewood Cliffs, New Jersey, Prentice-Hall.

Harris, I.C. (1991) 'How Environmentalist is Buddhism?', *Religion*, 21: 101–14.

Passmore, J. (1980) *Man's Responsibility for Nature*, London, Duckworth.

Ruegg, D.S. (1980) 'Ahimsa and Vegetarianism in the History of Buddhism', in Balasooriya, S. *et al.* (eds), *Buddhist Studies in Honour of Walpola Rahula*, London, Gordon Fraser.

White, L. Jnr (1967) 'The historical roots of our ecological crisis', *Science*, 155: 1204 ff.

2. Christianity

Douglas Davies

At first glance Christian attitudes to nature are relatively simple, so simple that western advertisers use images of crystal clear mountain streams, of natural mineral water, of healthy young people running free through woodlands or living in a flower-decked cottage in the countryside, to conjure up our sense of what is natural. And what is natural is believed to be good. But habits regarded by some people as perfectly natural are strongly opposed by others. There is, for example, some stiff opposition in Britain to the hunting of animals whether by people or dogs, as though this was an obviously bad practice despite the fact that hunting has been part of human behaviour for a very long time. Similarly, some people think it socially proper, physically healthy, and morally good, to be naked at what are called naturist clubs, while others think such behaviour morally questionable and even degrading.

These simple examples show how the word 'nature' comes with many built-in values and social conventions. Each society places its own relative emphasis upon natural things, so that what is true in one country may well be false in another. The British image of rural idylls with its attendant desire to own an historic country cottage is not entirely shared by the French, many of whom would prefer to live in modern houses in towns.

In this chapter we attempt to show how Christian ideas drawn from the Bible and its interpretation, as well as from church traditions, enter into our view of 'nature'. As we do this we will become aware of the interplay between various cultural views, some Christian and some non-Christian, which almost naturally seem to guide our outlook. As far as human beings are concerned, there seems to be no such thing as 'nature' existing as an untouched world of its own. Whether we see certain natural phenomena as pure and innocent or as red in tooth and claw depends upon the values and beliefs which human society brings to bear upon them. An understanding of nature requires an analysis of how cultures classify aspects of the world, and, in terms of Christian religion, it begins in the belief that God created all that is.

Creation

For Christian theology, attitudes to nature have been formed through the doctrine of creation, a doctrine grounded in the belief that the world is really there – surrounding us and forming our environment. Though this might seem a strange way to start discussing Christian attitudes to nature, it is nevertheless important because the reality of the world lies at the heart of all Christian theology.

THE REALITY OF NATURE IN CREATION

Central to the belief in the reality of the world is the conviction that when we open our eyes and look around us we are not deluded by what we see. The world of nature is no figment of our imagination, nor is it a trick played upon us by some supernatural being. The hard and fast reality of the universe and of our earth as part of it is guaranteed by the fact that God is responsible for it. Here, in God's responsibility, we have the first theological principle of creation. In traditional theological language, this prime responsibility of God is expressed through the slightly misleading Latin phrase *creatio ex nihilo*. This phrase, 'creation out of nothing', means that it is God who establishes and creates all things; it speaks of the primacy of God. It is precisely because God wills that the universe should exist and calls it into existence that we may speak of a further principle of creation, namely the dependable nature of the world. It was this dependability of nature that allowed later generations of scientists to study it in systematic ways, in the belief that the world would not change its nature between one day and another.

Initially, and in a fundamentally important way, Christianity drew heavily from the Hebrew scriptures when developing a doctrine of Creation and in coming to understand the wisdom of God in creation. In the Book of Genesis there are two accounts of creation. The first account, in Genesis (1: 1–2: 4), presents us with an orderly view of creation stemming from the Priestly tradition of Israel; at the outset God creates humanity as male and female. Following the pattern of a week, a day-by-day series of creative acts makes everything according to its kind. A similar Priestly motivation of order occurs in parts of the Books of Leviticus (ch. 1 ff.) and Deuteronomy (ch. 5 ff.), where a close parallel is drawn between the perfection of the natural world and the perfection of the social life to which God's people are called.

The second account of creation in Genesis (2: 4ff.), according to the Yahwistic tradition of Israel, starts from a different perspective and begins with the creation of the male. Only after a clear discussion of the loneliness of the man is woman produced from the male's rib.

The Priestly strand of the Hebrew scriptures accentuates both the careful orderliness of the world and the boundaries that surround Israel. Here it is difficult to separate the geographical territory of Israel from the social world of God's people, and to this we return shortly in exploring the symbolism of food taboos in Israel. Before that, it is worth stressing how relatively infrequently the idea of creation occurs throughout the rest of the Old Testament.

In the Wisdom literature of Psalms (74: 12–17 and 89: 5–12), in Proverbs (8: 22–31), in Job (38 and 39), and among the Prophets (Isa. 42: 5, 66: 1–2, Jer. 10: 12–13) there are some passages expressing God's power and responsibility as creator, but by far the greater number of references to God's creative power in the world preface a statement about God's right to be obeyed by Israel. An interesting feature of these accounts involves the place of humanity. Hebrew and Christian outlooks on creation always involve and implicate men and women within the total scheme.

Because writings in the Hebrew Bible were intended as expressions of social ideals and practical rules for a whole nation or people, they embrace aspects of life which are absent in the New Testament, which is aimed at a more restricted community of believers already existing within wider social frameworks.

RELATIONSHIPS AND RESPONSIBILITY

So it is that the Genesis portrayals of God's work describe the universe as a setting for human life. The universe is no neutral place. It is a place for men and women; but it is a place full of relationships and responsibilities. In fact these two words, relationship and responsibility, offer a direct way of grasping a Christian interpretation of the Hebrew idea of creation.

The very idea of relationships, whether between things, or people, or between people and God, provides the framework of creation in the first Genesis story. Everything is created according to its own kind and is related to all other kinds of things in an orderly way. In fact, orderly relationships constitute God's perfect world and in some senses reflect God's perfection. In the second creation story (Gen. 2.4 ff.), one heavily stressed relationship is that between human life and the very dust of the earth. People are left in no doubt that they came from, and will return to, the very earth itself – an idea which radically influences attitudes to the world and to nature. In powerful imagery, human beings are said to come from the dust of the earth in exactly the same way as do the animals. Because of this earthy origin, humanity and animals are portrayed as having a relationship with each other even though it is an unsatisfactory relationship as far as the human male is concerned. It is this very inadequacy that leads God to create woman out of man and, at the same time, to establish a new quality of relationship on the earth – that between man and woman.

So the doctrine of creation embraces not only the very ground itself along with plants, animals, and humans, but it also involves human relationships. In other words, social life is part and parcel of creation itself. So it is that no hard and fast line should ever be drawn between natural things and social things. For Christian theology, distinctions between nature and culture are inappropriate, a point to which we shall return later when considering theologies focusing on ecological and social issues.

The close relationship between nature and society is an important fact when we turn to the second key word in the Christian doctrine of creation – responsibility. Responsibility involves moral issues, and in the Hebrew scriptures it is closely linked to commandments. God commands Adam and Eve not to eat of the tree of the knowledge of good and evil (Gen. 2: 17). They quite simply disobey this command

and do not carry out their responsibilities towards God and his law. This act of disobedience, this irresponsibility, leads to a change in relationships. This whole situation is often referred to as the Fall, and depicts the moral weakness and flawed nature of men and women. In further strong imagery the woman is condemned to suffer pain in childbirth so that one of the most natural of acts is now to become a problem (Gen. 3: 16). In a very similar way men are to find their natural work of farming hard and strenuous (Gen. 3: 17–19).

So it is that the creation embraces a strong moral component. In the Hebrew scriptures all life possesses a moral dimension. Issues of good and evil surround all life, and are directly linked to the law and commandments of God. Here there is no possibility of looking in an abstract way at the world. Nature is not there simply to be appreciated; it is an arena of moral life speaking of God and involving God. Men and women cannot regard themselves simply as artists enjoying the world in a dispassionate sense, because the world is a vehicle for divine ends and is not an end in itself. Human beings are living members of a complex world, existing within all sorts of relationships with it and possessing all sorts of responsibilities towards it.

World and society

We have already said that the social world is part and parcel of creation. One of the clearest insights into this Hebrew view of the world comes from the idea of a promised land and a chosen people. Running throughout much of the Hebrew Bible is this deeply held belief that God had promised an actual territory to his own chosen people, and within it very particular areas for each of the major tribal clans (Num. 34). It was from this perspective of a divine society in a divine territory that the rest of the world made sense. And the rest of the world was not to be seen simply in geographical terms but also in terms of social life. One of the most important distinctions drawn in the Old Testament is between God's chosen people and those other nations who did not belong to that covenant community. These outsiders, or Gentiles (as non-Jews later came to be known), inhabited their own distinct territories so that, from the perspective of the Hebrew scriptures, as in most parts of the world today, geography and politics were practically the same thing.

As Christianity emerged from Jewish stock, it too, in the course of time, came to draw a distinction between members of the Christian community and outsiders not of the faith. Christianity also came to establish itself as a territorial religion, and it has not been unknown for some Christian groups to use the idea of a promised land as a way of thinking about God's will for them. A major way of looking at the world from one Christian perspective is indicated by the title 'Holy Roman Empire' that Charlemagne gave to his western empire on his coronation in 800 CE (an empire which lasted around 1,000 years until Napoleon brought it to a close in the early nineteenth century). Even in modern times we have become used to thinking of some societies as being Christian, Hindu, Muslim, Buddhist, Sikh, secular, or atheist. In other words, countries are still often categorised according to their dominant religious or ideological outlook.

Humans and animals in nature

We have already shown that the Jewish tradition argued that both humankind and animals originated from the dust of the ground and, because of that, shared a certain kinship. As a kind of analogy we might say that this joint origin in the Book of Genesis resembles the theory of evolution when it argues that humans and animals all come from pre-existing animal stock.

In the Hebrew Bible animals are distinguished from one another in several ways. In the first Genesis creation myth, sea creatures are distinguished from the birds, both of which were said to be created in the fifth day. Beasts, cattle, creeping things and humankind were all created on the sixth day, as distinct groups. Humanity is given a distinct command to be fruitful and fill the earth, to subdue it and to have dominion over these various animal groups. It is a dominion that follows from the fact, clearly linked in the text, that male and female were created in the image of God (Gen. 1: 27,28).

In the various laws associated with the running of God's ideal society, those animals that may be regarded as domesticated have certain rights afforded to them. An individual should, for example, assist an ox or an ass that has fallen. Even a bird's nest with eggs, young, and mother should be treated with due care; the eggs may be taken but the mother must be allowed to remain free (Deut. 22: 4, 6–7).

Unclean animals and food

In the Books of Leviticus (11: 2–23) and Deuteronomy (14: 3–20) fixed rules are given as to which animals may or may not be eaten by Jews. These rules are interesting, showing as they do just how closely attitudes to nature are linked to religious ideas. Although these rules have been interpreted by biblical scholars in different ways, one of the most suggestive explanations of why they exist came from the British social anthropologist, Mary Douglas.

She argued that the picture of the world drawn out in the Levitical and Deuteronomic codes of life is one of order and tight control. There was a place for everything, and when everything was in its place the overall harmonious picture of society reflected and symbolised the unity of God. Social order expressed divine order. Orderliness had a strong moral dimension – order was good, chaos was bad. This was all the more important, given the fact that Israel was much concerned with its identity as God's people. Marriage, for example, should be with members and not with outsiders. All of which led to a preoccupation with boundaries of behaviour.

This is where the rules for eating come in as a sort of perpetual reminder and symbol of the good order, because those creatures deemed unclean for eating had something about them which indicated disorder or chaos. The pig, for example, is classified as unclean because it has a cloven hoof but does not chew the cud (Deut. 14: 8). The logic of this prohibition is that animals which have cloven hoofs and also chew the cud are like the normal grazing animals familiar to the tribes of Israel; such animals express the good order of society. But the pig possesses only half the qualification for inclusion in that normal category; in that sense the pig is an anomaly. It shares the features of two different categories of creature, and because it straddles the boundary line it is a bad example of perfection. In a similar way, if anything comes from river or sea and has fins and scales as do ordinary fish, then it is clean. But anything that comes from the water and lacks such 'fishy' signs is deemed unclean (Deut. 14: 9–10).

This sort of interpretation can be extended to explain why the Jews were commanded not to weave two types of cloth together, nor plough using a donkey and an ox (Deut. 22: 10–11). In all aspects of life everything should be 'according to its kind' as the first creation myth expresses the orderliness of creation, for that order helps distinguish God's people from other nations, and also expresses the divine orderliness of God. Here there can be no attitude towards nature that is not at the same time an attitude towards society and, indirectly, towards God.

This point becomes extremely clear in the symbolism of Peter's dream in the Acts of the Apostles (Acts 10: 9 ff.), where there is presentation of the Old Testament food law which is immediately transcended. Peter has a vision of food which is unclean. When told to eat it he recoils, saying that he has never eaten anything that is unclean. The answer that comes to him is very powerful, saying that what God has cleansed none should call unclean. The clear implication is that former rules of a closed society and a closed religion are now overcome, as the Christian religion opens the way for all to come and worship God. Immediately afterwards Peter is summoned to preach to the Gentiles.

In its subsequent history, Christianity has been remarkably open on the matter of food. We might even say that because Christianity emerged from Judaism and possesses a very clear abandonment of the Old Testament food regulations, it was easy for it not to fall into extensive new food rules. One consequence of this is that Christianity has had relatively few food problems as a missionary movement entering new cultures.

Scripture, worship and nature

The belief that God's creation of nature is a cause of worship and praise is already found in the Jewish scriptures, and furnished Christianity with a fundamentally important view of the universe. A few of the Psalms dwell quite specifically on the wonders of God's work in nature. Psalm 104 expresses the idea of God's wise creativity at some length. It is a creativity that stimulates the human response of worship. God it is who stretches out the heavens, establishes the earth, causes grass to grow, gives the sea its depth and fills it with creatures. God it is who gives life to all things and who ultimately takes away their breath of life, causing them to return to the dust of the earth. As men and women ponder these facts they praise and bless God. The world of nature is a world in which the Christian, like the Jew, takes delight precisely because it is an expression of God's will and power. The Psalms are one particular source of such worship: 'The heavens declare the glory of

God', begins Psalm 19, before it goes on to say how both day and night and the sun expressly obey the divine command. But it is true to say that throughout the Psalms, as also in the Book of Job (38–41), practically every mention of natural phenomena is associated with their divine originator. Very little biblical material dwells on nature as such. Nature exists not in its own right but as a created entity. Humanity may appreciate it and use it, but never focus solely on it.

Another aspect of creation reinforces this point: the world stands as a witness to God over against humanity. In early Christianity Paul speaks of this invisible power, and of God as being revealed in and through the visible aspects of the world. He even argues that humans are without an excuse for not believing in God precisely because the visible world should leave them in no doubt about God's existence (Rom. 1: 19–20). Subsequent Christians, such as Augustine (354–430 CE), could speak of the world as a kind of great book written by God but with real objects in the place of words.

It is here that human beings can easily look at nature, or read it, in a wrong way and, instead of praising God because of it, see it as an end in itself and become idolators. The worship of nature is fundamentally wrong for Christians because created things are put in the place properly belonging to the creator. Paul, in the same early section of his Letter to the Romans, speaks in just this way about people worshipping and serving the creature rather than the creator (1: 19–25). So it is that, biblically speaking, there is no such thing as an attitude to nature devoid of a parallel attitude to God, its creator.

While the natural world may cause men and women to reflect on God and to turn their minds in a divine direction, as in Psalm 19 where the heavens are said to declare the glory of God, Christian theology has always maintained a sharp distinction between God and the created order. Some mystical trends occasionally employ the idea of pantheism to suggest that God is one with the universe, as the philosopher Spinoza (1632–77) had argued. Orthodox theology has denied this on the basis that God was transcendent. Perhaps one of the reasons why humankind often talks about itself as distinct from nature is because Christian men and women see themselves related to the world in a similarly separate way. Even here theological ideas help influence attitudes to natural realities.

Flawed but renewable

Although the Bible emphasises the reality of the world, it also argues that this very real world is not what it should be. The first Genesis story of creation depicts God looking upon the creation and pronouncing it to be very good (Gen. 1: 31). But, as we shall see in more detail later, with the sinful disobedience of humanity, the world is cursed. This theme recurs in the words of the Prophets, who see God blessing the world when the chosen people are obedient and blighting it when they are disobedient. This theme is developed in some of the Books of the Prophets, with the divine promise to make new heavens and a new earth in which perfection will exist. This sense of perfection involves the obedience of God's people and also a world of justice and orderly life with all chaos removed – a place where 'the wolf and the lamb shall feed together, the lion shall eat straw like the ox' (Isa. 65: 25).

Christians adopted much of this Jewish approach to the physical world, both in seeing the present order as imperfect and in believing that God would transform it in the last days. One strand of New Testament teaching speaks of Christians as 'waiting for new heavens and a new earth in which righteousness dwells' (2 Pet. 3: 13). Biblical teaching about such a final period, or eschatology as it has been called over the last century and a half, binds the destiny of believers close to the destiny of the world. Paul's important contribution in his Letter to the Romans speaks of the creation as being caught up in a process of decay. He speaks as though the creation is caught in the painful pangs of birth. Believer and world together are prisoners, and groan as they seek release. But the hope is sure, and the 'glorious liberty of the children of God' will come to believer and to the world (Rom. 8: 21). But perhaps the best known description of this Christian longing comes in the Book of Revelation. There the visionary sees a new heaven and a new earth following on from the old heaven and earth which had passed away. Central to the vision is a new Jerusalem which comes down to the new earth and is the centre of divine blessing for humankind. As we show at several points in this chapter, New Jerusalem is both a city and a garden. It combines within itself images of the old Jerusalem and of the garden of Eden. A river of life flows through its central street, which is bordered by the tree of life (Rev. 22: 2).

This clear vision of a renewed world has seldom played a central part in mainstream Christian thinking, but some sectarian movements have focused on it in a very powerful way. In the mid- and late nineteenth century the Mormons in Utah saw their own geographical area as a special place to which God had led them. By their hard work and careful social organisation, arid land was becoming very fruitful. In biblical terms, following Isaiah (35: 1), they saw the desert blossoming as a rose and becoming a new kind of promised land. Once more the idea of a promised land went hand in hand with their belief in themselves as a chosen people.

In the twentieth century, the Jehovah's Witnesses stressed the wrongness of the present system of things in the world, and testified to their belief that it would take a major act of God to restore the world to the divine plan. In many ways the Mormon and Jehovah's Witness examples illustrate the 'this-worldly' orientation of biblical religion, which many central Christian views had forgotten in their growing tendency to see salvation in terms of the destiny of the human soul in heaven after this earthly life is ended.

Nature and heaven

There have been tendencies in Christianity to draw a line between sacred and secular aspects of life, and to view nature in a negative light. The contrast between spirit and flesh was used by Paul in his Letter to the Romans (8: 5) and appears in a similar way in the First Letter of John, where Christians are exhorted not to love the world or the things in the world (1 John 2: 15). In an interesting way, we find that the first two Christian centuries show little concern with asceticism. Instead, there is a basic acceptance of the world. It is only in the third century that asceticism begins to make its presence felt. By the time of Ambrose of Milan, in the fourth century, asceticism assumes a major significance, so much so that virginity is deemed superior to the married state. Marriage becomes one formal expression of worldly life as opposed to spiritual existence, a distinction that is not intrinsic to the Bible itself.

The more directly biblical distinction between flesh and spirit is reflected, for example, in the fifth century, when Augustine followed a similar path in *The City of God*, where his two cities depicted two loves – of God and of self. Such a spirit–flesh distinction, even though it does not refer directly to aspects of nature, is a view that encourages asceticism and sees the spiritual life in a rather narrow way. Some traditions, where monks and nuns have remained unmarried and live quite apart from the ordinary world, illustrate this distinction between spirit and flesh which comes to match a distinction between heaven and earth. For such people, the truly religious life is lived on the border between earth and heaven, and this is why regular worship in churches was so important.

Another tradition within Christianity has taken a quite different approach, affirming a 'this-worldly' rather than an 'other-worldly' perspective. There have been religious orders which have stressed this perspective, as in the modern case of Mother Teresa and her nuns. In the twentieth century this strongly affirmative outlook has been emphasised both by Liberation theologians in their stress on social justice, and by theologians with ecological concerns to care for world resources. Before considering this very recent Ecological theology, in the next part of this chapter we will explore one major theological concern which prepared the ground for these recent developments.

Incarnational theology and nature

Christianity has, formally, spent more time discussing human nature than it has the nature of animals, plants, or the cosmos. There are some exceptions to this and, for example, the historian Keith Thomas has shown how popular religion in Britain often regarded animals as capable of having some sort of religion. Indeed, in the period after the Reformation it was argued by some that animals could gain immortality (Thomas, 1984: 137 ff.). Even so, in modern theology attitudes to nature have often ignored animals and plants, and focused on human nature and on the precise identity of Jesus of Nazareth. In one very real sense, then, Christian attitudes to nature focus on attitudes towards Jesus. This is very clear in the history of doctrine which, over the first five centuries of Christian history, was preoccupied with the relationship between human nature and divine nature within the one person of Jesus.

Christian orthodoxy came to be formulated through great Councils of church leaders, as at Nicea (325 CE) and Chalcedon (451 CE). Central to their conclusions was the belief that Jesus was fully human and also fully divine, a single person possessing two natures. This was believed to be important for Christian theology, to ensure the salvation of men and women: because their full humanity had been assumed by Jesus, it had also been redeemed through him. There was a deep awareness of this need for human nature to be fully entered into and taken on by Jesus before human beings could be saved from sin. This was the generally accepted position of orthodoxy. Implicit in this belief was that God loved human beings enough to become one of them in Jesus of Nazareth. Human nature had now become associated with divine nature in the person of one individual. This meant that human beings could reflect on their own identity through the belief that God had not only created humanity but had also entered into humanity. This divine approval or validation of human nature, in the very process of salvation, gave to men and women the opportunity of looking positively on their own life and its significance.

Because God had assumed humanity in one concrete individual, it was now not only perfectly proper, but also necessary, for all Christians to look on other people in a more profound way (2 Cor. 5: 15–19). So it is that attitudes to human nature are forged not only through the doctrine of creation, but also through the doctrine of redemption.

This process of God entering into humanity in the individual man, Jesus of Nazareth, is spoken of in theology as the doctrine of the Incarnation. It is a doctrine closely associated in Christian belief with what is often called sacramental theology, emphasising how ordinary aspects of life can be endowed with religious significance. This refers not only to official church sacraments using wine, bread, or water as in the eucharist or baptism, but to many other aspects of life, and in one sense it embraces the very matter of the universe itself. In this incarnational-sacramental theology, God employs natural phenomena as vehicles for religious truth. For Christians committed to this view of the universe, attitudes to nature are grounded in a world of divine value and significance.

Evolution

Religious values have not, however, been the sole influence on people's interpretation of the world, and religious ideas themselves changed shape because of the impact of other philosophical and scientific ideas. Because the Christian religion has been closely bound up with the total cultural life of Europe for at least the last 1,500 years, it is quite understandable that major shifts in general thought are reflected in religious thinking, just as theological thought makes its own impact upon wider social currents. In looking at some of these changes and influences as they affect attitudes to nature, we shall look first at some nineteenth- and twentieth-century issues before returning to the sixteenth century. We do this because one of the most important changes in human self-understanding is rooted in Darwin's work in the mid-nineteenth century.

In 1859 Charles Darwin (1808–82) published *The Origin of Species*, and in 1871, *The Descent of Man*. These biological studies reinforced the more speculative philosophical and sociological work of scholars like Herbert Spencer (1820–1902) and caused much debate in the last third of the nineteenth century.

The basic problem was that traditional Christian thought, like thought in general, believed that God had created human beings, fully formed and identifiably human, shortly after the creation of the world of nature. Darwin's biological theory of evolution combined with the findings of geologists to argue that the world was very much older than traditional theology had assumed, and that human beings had emerged from pre-human forms of animal life. More than this, his idea of the survival of the fittest implied that divine will and providence were not the cause behind the emergence of men and women. Natural biological processes were the fundamental processes of life.

Some nineteenth-century Christians regarded this theory of evolution as quite antagonistic to Christianity, as witnessed in a debate at Oxford in 1860, when the bishop of that diocese, Samuel Wilberforce, tried to ridicule the idea of evolution but was himself politely humbled by the scientist, T.H. Huxley. A few nineteenth-century Christians, such as F.B. Jevons (1858–1936) of Durham, warmly accepted evolutionary theories and saw them as complementing the doctrine of creation. It was in this later nineteenth-century period that Christian approaches to nature were challenged and stimulated into new thinking about God and the world.

These questions are still important, because some Christians think there is a sharp distinction between the doctrine of creation and the theory of evolution. At its simplest, this argument sets the intentional creative act of God in opposition to the accidental or random event of the origin of the universe with the subsequent evolution of life. Intention versus accident is a key distinction here and no compromise is believed to be possible between the two world views.

EVOLUTION AS CREATION

Another view, adopted by some Christians, accepts the general process of evolution but assumes that the universe itself, however it came into existence, was intended by God. The origin of the cosmos and the evolution of life on earth are both seen as part of God's overall creative scheme. Here evolution is creation. Ultimately, this view does not accept that the existence of life is accidental and random. The Catholic priest and scientist, Pierre Teilhard de Chardin (1881–1955), developed his own modern religious philosophy of creation from an evolutionary perspective. Central to it was the belief that Christ was the centre of love for our cosmos which is a dynamic system of interrelationships; even matter is endued with a degree of dynamic awareness. Christ is the focus and goal for human existence, making sense of the past as well as providing hope for the future. Much of Teilhard de Chardin's language and terminology was unacceptable to the church authorities of his day, who prevented him from publishing his work and sent him to work in China for long periods. It is also unacceptable to most scientists. Even so, Teilhard de Chardin shows the importance of evolution and of Christ for a modern Christian perception of the world. He shows how important it is to consider theological issues in the light of scientific knowledge and to strive seriously to integrate them. Some problems are inevitably caused by such thinkers, because older forms of argument and older patterns of theology cannot quite cope with new insights. One important example of this concerns sin.

Nature, sin and evolution

As we saw earlier, one major stream of traditional Christian theology speaks of sin in relation to the Fall of humankind. God's perfect creation comes to be spoiled through the disobedience of humanity, as in chapter three of the Book of Genesis, where the very ground is cursed to produce weeds because of Adam's wickedness. One consequence of this approach is that the world of nature is viewed as a sorry scene. The golden age is in the past and only in some future age will it be restored in heaven, or in some dramatic act of the last days. There is little place in this tradition for a view of evolutionary development of the world and its moral nature.

This scheme of a Fall in the past and some future divine

restoration belongs to a world view which tends to take some aspects of Genesis and of the Book of Revelation as literally true. It reminds us that the question of creation and evolution often involves a very particular kind of biblical interpretation – one that stresses the literal truth of biblical passages.

Views which give an important place to evolutionary ideas will almost certainly not follow that kind of literal path, which focuses on a very few passages of scripture. Instead they will draw from numerous aspects of the Bible and other Christian traditions of doctrine, interpreted in non-literal ways.

This is true for what has been called Process theology. Following the philosophy of A.N. Whitehead (1861–1947), Process theologians have interpreted the world as a developing and dynamic reality, intimately related to God and progressing in such a way that God's love increasingly comes to the fore (Pittinger, 1967). The stress on love is related to a strong emphasis upon human personality and its development, not only within the individual but throughout history and human culture. Events in the here and now are also given pride of place in order to emphasise the on-going process of evolution. It is the task of men and women to engage themselves with this on-going work of creation, to ensure that love increasingly influences human life. In this scheme of things, sin and evil can be understood as hindrances and backward movements in the process of world creation. In Process thought, both the idea of love and the idea of evil demonstrate the intimate association of human beings with the material world (Ogden, 1967). Process theology makes an important contribution to a Christian understanding of nature by arguing that human life is part and parcel of the universe itself, sharing in the shaping of the world for the future. Natural and moral values are closely combined, just as God is intimately involved in the evolving world of nature and humanity. Here there is no place for a sharp distinction between the world and the church. Historically, this link between theology and science has not always been so obvious and easy, as was particularly true in the sixteenth century.

The universe, God and orthodoxy

The sixteenth century was a period of astonishing change as far as western Christendom was concerned. Part of this change deeply affected attitudes to nature. The religious reformation of Martin

Luther (1483–1546) was matched by the scientific revolution inaugurated by Nicolas Copernicus (1473–1543). Copernicus came to the conclusion that the earth moved round the sun. For us, today, this idea is accepted as an ordinary fact of life, but it has not always been the case. This simple change of outlook was to be radically important in giving humanity a different sense of its own importance. Instead of being the inhabitants of the centre of the universe, human beings could now see themselves as resident upon a subsidiary and peripheral planet.

This changed view of the universe necessarily involved a change in the view of the world. Subsequent astronomers and physicists reinforced this new perception of the universe. Sometimes, as in the work of Johannes Kepler (1571–1630), who formulated some basic laws explaining the movement of the planets, these new interpretations were linked with theological ideas. Kepler, for example, thought that the orderliness of nature expressed something of the nature of God. He saw analogies between the sun as God the Father, the fixed stars and God the Son, and the realm of the moving planets and God the Spirit. The orderliness of the universe was something that appealed strongly to another profoundly religious scientist, Isaac Newton (1642–1727). His discovery of the law of gravity is well known, but it is also worth remembering his religious convictions, which were not always orthodox. Not only did he find the doctrine of the Holy Trinity rather contrary to reason, but also he was much given to speculation on millenarian ideas about the end of the world.

The emergence of scientific ideas influencing our view of the world has, occasionally, led to major opposition from church authorities. We have already seen this with Darwin's evolutionary theories in the nineteenth century. But there was a far starker conflict in the early seventeenth century when the astronomer Galileo (1564–1642), who incidentally discovered four satellites of Jupiter with his new invention of the astronomical telescope, forcefully argued the Copernican theory of the sun's centrality to our universe. The Catholic Church took exception to his utterances and formally condemned the Copernican theory in 1616. The Church still affirmed and supported the traditional Ptolemaic view of the universe, where everything revolved around the earth. Galileo was summoned to Rome, was subjected to the Inquisition and forced to recant under threat of torture. His support of the Copernican theory was regarded as a form of heresy. After nearly a decade, he was permitted to return to Florence, where he died. After his recantation he is reckoned to have added words to the effect that, 'it does move all the same'. This episode in the history of science is at the same time a moment in the history of theology, showing how attitudes to nature are intrinsically linked with theological beliefs about creation. It also opens up the meaning of the word 'nature', showing that it embraces our total understanding of the universe and not simply what we think about animal rights or ecology.

Many aspects of thought in the seventeenth and, especially, eighteenth centuries emphasised human reason in arriving at a sense of what the world was about. One strand of thought discussed the place of humankind within the broad flow of nature, or the great chain of being, and argued that there was a kind of principle of continuity, with all parts of the world being filled with appropriate creatures. This philosophical outlook prepared the way for the nineteenth century's more scientific discovery of the theory of evolution.

But perhaps the Scottish philosopher, David Hume (1711–76), can be taken as a more typical exponent of the eighteenth century age of reason, in which the world of nature was very largely given a secondary place because of the preoccupation with human thought and human knowledge. As a response to the alienation of humankind from nature inherent within the age of reason, we witness at the close of the eighteenth century the rise of Romanticism – a general outlook which brought the world of nature back into the forefront of experience and thought. It is not surprising that the Romantics, like Wordsworth (1770–1850), used poetry to express the power and significance of nature in sharp contrast to the logical, philosophical treatises of the rationalists.

One important aspect of Romantic thought is the belief that nature impresses upon human beings a sense of the significance and unity of things – a kind of sense of presence. Nature is perceived as dynamic and is not simply there as an object to be observed. Some of Wordsworth's thoughts expressed in his *Lines Composed a few Miles Above Tintern Abbey* touch on this outlook:

> And I have felt
> A presence that disturbs me with the joy
> Of elevated thoughts: a sense sublime

> Of something far more deeply interfused,
> Whose dwelling is the light of setting suns,
> And the round ocean and the living air . . .

This outlook is not far removed from that of mystical religious individuals who prefer to speak of encountering God through nature rather than of having some sort of objective view of nature. The material world becomes the arena within which a knowledge of God is born and expands, so much so that the believer may feel quite at one with all that is. At such a moment, the world of nature is the means by which the believer reckons to gain an intuitive knowledge of reality. Before the Romantics, the seventeenth-century English mystic, Thomas Traherne (1637–74), could say:

> You never Enjoy the World aright till the Sea itself floweth in your Veins, till you are Clothed with the Heavens, and Crowned with the Stars . . . till you delight in God for being Good to all.
>
> (*Centuries of Meditations*, 1: 29)

A secular dynamic world

Within broad Christian culture it is important to consider the ideas of those who do not start from a theological, or even from any official Christian, standpoint because of the mutual influences which always seem to be at work in society. J.E. Lovelock, for example, published a book in 1979 that has become influential in discussions of ecology and human responsibility for the world (Lovelock, 1979). He called his book *Gaia* after the Greek goddess of the earth, a suggestion made to him by his novelist neighbour, William Golding. *Gaia* is subtitled, 'A New Look at Life on Earth', and is really a hypothesis about the world we inhabit. The hypothesis is that the actual chemical and physical nature of the earth's surface, its atmosphere and oceans, has been brought about by the presence of life itself. More than that, it is a self-regulating system with a capacity to keep the world as a healthy system capable of sustaining life. In this sense it is an intelligent system. It also embraces humanity.

In Lovelock's outlook, many people have an implicit understanding of the fact that life is one immense system of interlinked parts. This reflects a kind of long-standing folk-wisdom or paganism which the churches do not like to admit still exists. Even so, Lovelock suggests that the churches, along with humanist movements, have come to see the power of environmental campaigns and have revised their own theology to catch up with the mood of the age. He particularly criticises the continuing Christian concern to stress humankind's stewardship of the world, because he sees in this a continued desire to keep humans centre stage. With this in mind, it is interesting that one popular book on Christian faith in relation to nature was entitled *To Care for the Earth* (McDonagh, 1986), a title reflecting the Christian sense of responsibility for the world alongside the centrality of men and women within it. Its author, Sean McDonagh, was well aware of the Gaia hypothesis and argued for the emergence of a Christian spirituality developed from a modern understanding of the earth. But still the commitment to the Christian idea of human importance comes to the fore, as is, perhaps, inevitable in the light of the doctrine of creation. For Lovelock, by subtle contrast, men and women along with all other animals, plants and chemical systems, exist together in a mutual overall system of things which is Gaia. There is no precedence accorded to humankind, even though it may be that human intellect and technology will, in the future, be able to help the total system of nature to protect itself.

In terms of Christian theology, it is practically impossible not to see humanity as central to the world of nature. This is because of the fundamental distinction between the Christian belief that God willed and intended a world of which humankind should be a part, and that kind of scientific interpretation which sees the emergence of the cosmos, of the earth and, ultimately, of life, as accidental. We have already mentioned this distinction between intention and accident, but its importance demands a re-emphasis, since it is this sharp difference between an intended and an accidental universe which stands at the centre of the religion and science debate over the universe. Some Christians wish to stress this divide and to sharpen the distinction between the creative will of God and the accidental events of matter. There are some, especially in the USA, who actively oppose the theory of evolution precisely because they see it as godless. They press other Christians not to accept evolutionary theories because to do so is to deny belief in the divine will to create the world. For these individuals, a Christian view of nature, often based on a literal understanding of the Book of Genesis, necessitates a clear belief that God willed the world into existence in a clearly intentional way. They do not wish their children to be taught evolutionary theory in school because they see that as a form of secular indoctrination and contrary to Christianity.

Other Christians, probably the majority, accept the theory of evolution but bring to it a theological assumption. They, too, start with the belief that God is fundamentally responsible for the universe, the earth and humankind, but they accept evolutionary processes in a qualified form by arguing that these are the means by which God creates things. We have already seen this in the work of Teilhard de Chardin. An English scientist and theologian, A.R. Peacocke (1971), has also argued, more recently, on the assumption that evolutionary processes are fundamental to the way God continually creates the universe.

One idea of real interest to several contemporary scientists and theologians has been called the anthropic principle. This idea argues that human self-consciousness is not an accident of the evolutionary process but that the very way life-systems are organised in the universe is such as to produce humankind. Another related issue is the fact that the world is so intelligible in terms of physics and mathematics. In fact, mathematicians and physicists often seem to speak of the universe as a far more intelligible place than do philosophers and scholars of literature.

What these various arguments from science and religion show is that Christian attitudes to nature are not simply concerned with such things as the beauty of flowers but with the meaning of the universe itself. Christian theology deals with this immense question of the meaning of the universe in philosophical ways, as we have already shown, but for many believers the theme is also pursued through the medium of worship in what may be called a celebration of nature.

Celebrating nature

Because many Christians understand and express their faith more through worship than through formal theology, it is wise not to ignore attitudes to nature developed through worship. So, although we have already mentioned some Psalms in relation to the doctrine of creation, we now go on to look at other canticles and hymns which have given expression to Christian perspectives.

One of the longest-standing hymns of praise to God, which

celebrates nature and calls upon natural phenomena to worship God, is the *Benedicite*. This latin title (bless ye) begins a hymn of praise put into the mouths of the three men in a fiery furnace in the Jewish *Song of The Three*. It has been used in Christian ritual from very early days and was widespread in Europe by the fifth century. In the Church of England, for example, it stands as a canticle in the service of Morning Prayer in The Book of Common Prayer. It embraces many aspects of nature:

> O all ye works of the Lord, bless ye the Lord:
> Praise him, and magnify him for ever.
> O ye sun and moon . . . stars of heaven . . . showers and dew . . . winds . . . winter and summer . . . frost and cold . . .
> O all ye green things upon the earth . . .
> Whales . . . fowls of the air . . . beasts and cattle . . .
> Praise him and magnify him for ever.

A very similar message runs through the hymn, 'All creatures of our God and King', which is based on St Francis of Assisi's 'Canticle of the Sun', from the early thirteenth century. Francis is renowned as a Christian whose simple life involved a closeness to animals and nature, and some Christians have recently heralded him as a prophet of ecological theology. It is always unwise to force or project the issues and problems of one generation back on to another, and this is probably also true of Francis, whose sense of unity with natural things was not prompted by worries over survival (cf. R.D. Sorrell, 1988), but by a sense of common purpose and fulfilment in the service of God. This is clearly expressed in 'All creatures of our God and King', where sun and moon, wind, and flowing water, along with mother earth and her flowers, are all called upon to praise and worship God.

HARVEST THANKSGIVING

A few more recent hymns of the eighteenth and nineteenth centuries have focused on 'the little flowers and birds', but usually in hymns for children, such as 'All things bright and beautiful, all creatures great and small' of 1848. More frequently, however, attention is fixed on the harvest and the relation of the natural elements to harvest. 'We plough the fields, and scatter the good seed on the land', is a favourite hymn of many churches. It was written in the late eighteenth century, and always used at Harvest Festival or Harvest Thanksgiving Services in Britain. It expresses the rural nature of much European and North American Protestant religion, and summarises human response to God for the produce of nature:

> All good gifts around us
> Are sent from heaven above;
> Then thank the Lord, O thank the Lord,
> For all His love.

Even so, this hymn, like the similar 'Come, ye thankful people, come', is an agricultural hymn. Both focus on cultivated fields rather than on wild animals and plants. God's providence is connected with the supply of food, and in this sense the attitude to nature is an extension of human need. It is interesting that Harvest Thanksgiving Services are relatively modern as church-based events in the UK. Although secular celebration of harvest had long occurred in Britain, as in most agricultural societies, it became specifically linked with the church only in the nineteenth century.

In 1843 the Vicar of Morwenstow in Cornwall developed and extended a custom relating to Lammas Day in late summer, when the bread for Holy Communion was baked from new corn that had just been harvested. This church-focused custom became increasingly popular, with the decoration of churches with corn, fruit, vegetables and flowers. By 1862, the Church of England had produced a form of service for the occasion. As time went on, and especially in industrial towns and cities, other aspects of human endeavour, such as coal or manufactured products, were often added to the harvest goods as an expression of human work and of thanks to God.

Whether dealing with harvest or nature in general, these hymns are few in number. Most traditional hymnbooks have more hymns on heaven and the afterlife than they do on earth and the environment of nature. This is fully in accord with the fact that Christianity's overarching concern has, traditionally, been more with the salvation of individuals couched in terms of church membership and the world of heaven rather than the protection of earth's ecology.

Animal rights

Among the few theologians whose attitude to nature struck a distinctively different note is Albert Schweitzer (1875–1965). He was one of the most remarkable scholars of the twentieth century, having made important contributions to philosophical, biblical and musical scholarship. After all that, he learned medicine and became a medical missionary in Africa. In his volumes on the philosophy of civilisation, Schweitzer developed the idea of what he called 'reverence for life'. This concern, which embraced the belief that even insects should be respected and not killed, is strange as far as Christianity is concerned, being a more distinctive feature of Buddhism. Even so, this man, who was awarded a Nobel Peace Prize, did emphasise and seek to practise reverence for nature – a strange phrase, given the fact that Christians normally use reverence only in respect of God. For Schweitzer it was something of a passion, and stemmed from a personal conviction that had dawned upon him in a radically profound way. It was more of an ethical motive for life than any sort of celebration of nature.

In many respects it is this ethical aspect of attitudes to nature that has come to predominate in western countries in this last third of the twentieth century. The very idea of animal rights stands in the tradition of ethical concerns over which religious values have had such an influence. But the major concern for animal rights has tended not to originate specifically within theology, but from wider public opinion and pressure groups such as the World Wide Fund for Nature (formerly the World Wildlife Fund) and Greenpeace. The protection of endangered species has been a major concern on the ethical basis that it is wrong for humanity to destroy another species. Concern for giant pandas, dolphins and whales has been accentuated through extensive media coverage, and has led to many people gaining a knowledge of the way of life of these animals far beyond former levels of popular awareness.

Another attitude to nature that has also developed more recently within traditionally Christian western societies is vegetarianism. Vegetarianism enshrines for many the belief that it is wrong to be cruel to animals by farming them intensively and then slaughtering them just for food. There is no strictly theological or biblical basis for vegetarianism or for this attitude in Christianity, but it can be viewed as an extension of the ideal of love. The growth of animal rights follows on from an immense increase in awareness of human rights, seen throughout the twentieth century, and shows how attitudes to nature are intimately bound up with attitudes to human nature – and ultimately to theological beliefs about the human condition.

FURTHER READING

Douglas, M. (1966) *Purity and Danger*, London, Routledge & Kegan Paul.

Hendry, G.S. (1980) *Theology of Nature*, Philadelphia, Westminster Press.

Lovelock, J.E. (1979) *Gaia: A New Look at Life on Earth*, Oxford, Oxford University Press.

McDonagh, S. (1986) *To Care for the Earth*, London, Chapman.

Ogden, S.M. (1967) *The Reality of God and Other Essays*, London, S.C.M. Press.

Peacocke, A.R. (1971) *Science and the Christian Experiment*, Oxford, Oxford University Press.

Pittinger, N. (1967) *God in Process*, London, S.C.M. Press.

Sorrell, R.D. (1988) *St. Francis of Assisi*, New York, Oxford University Press.

Thomas, K. (1984) *Man and the Natural World*, London, Penguin.

3. Hinduism

Anuradha Roma Choudhury

Hinduism is not a religion in the formal western sense of the term. There is no single founder, so no accountable time when it started. There is revealed scripture, but no single Holy Book prescribed. Instead, there are innumerable names of sages (*ṛṣis*) and saints passed down through centuries as contributors to this collective idea called Hinduism, and several philosophical works composed in different ages considered significant enough to become the body of the scriptures.

It follows that, in discussing Hindu[1] understandings of nature, we come across a wide range of ideas: on the one hand, we find ideas which reflect very early human encounters with natural phenomena, such as we find elsewhere in the world (i.e., the initial sense of awe and humility towards the natural forces), and on the other hand, we find lofty philosophical ideas which undoubtedly are the product of a mature analytical mind.

In the early period, numerous invaders or settlers entered India from outside. Among them, the Aryan (*Ārya*) contributed most to the Hindu way of life. They brought with them their well-developed language, Sanskrit (*Saṃskṛta*), their ritual worship, their sacrificial fire. The world's oldest literature, the Vedas (*veda* meaning knowledge), followed by the *Brāhmaṇa*s, *Āraṇyaka*s and *Upaniṣad*s, are the product of the Aryan intellect.

From the scriptural literature it is evident that the initial urge for appeasing the forces of nature with rituals and hymns of prayer gradually turned into a quest for unravelling the mysteries of nature. Out of adoration for nature, grew a faithful search for a Creator, the cause or root of this magnificent creation. From this search evolved Hindu theories of cosmology: the universe, its creation and dissolution. Several schools of philosophy developed as the mature analytical mind probed deeper into the secrets of nature and also attempted to establish a relationship between the created phenomena and their creator.

To get the complete picture of how Hindus view nature, one has to consider two perspectives. One is the wider perspective of the creation as a whole – the universe, its stars and planets, and its relationship with its creator; and the other is the intimate perspective of the Mother Earth – her plants and animals, and her relationship with the humans.

Concept of creation (*sṛṣṭi*)

As with other early civilisations, very basic questions were addressed: How is the world created? Who is the Creator? Is there a Creator? In answering these questions each civilisation created its own theories of cosmology in general and cosmogony in particular. Many of them assume that the phenomenal world, despite its apparent permanence, did not exist throughout eternity. It had an origin at a certain time in the past and it would go into oblivion at some future date. Like mortal beings, the world too has been born and is destined to die.

The Hindu thinkers went a step further, and stated that the universe has no single birth nor an ultimate death. The creation and dissolution of the universe is a cyclical on-going process. A variety of sources is available in the sacred writings to show the kinds of attempts made through the ages, both in vedic and non-vedic fields, to explain how an individual creation takes place and how it goes into oblivion.

The early speculations to resolve the mystery of creation refer back to records which were pure myths. To start with a non-vedic cosmological myth, the narrative of *Śrī Chaṇḍī* (a part of the *Mārkaṇḍeya Purāṇa*) (I 66–104) states that the universe, prior to the creation, was filled with *kāraṇa-salila* (*kāraṇa*/cause, *salila*/water/fluid), or causal/primordial fluid. In the infinite expanse of primordial fluid, Nārāyaṇa, the Supreme Being, was lying in deep slumber (*yoga-nidrā*) on the coils of *Ananta-Nāga* (*ananta*/infinite, *nāga*/snake; stands symbolically for infinite dimension of time length). A lotus (*padma* – often associated with mystic symbolism) sprang up from the navel of Nārāyaṇa (also known as Viṣṇu). Over the lotus was seated Brahmā, the deity who, according to puranic legendary heritage,[2] is considered to be the creator. Next, two demons (*asuras*) emerged from Nārāyaṇa's *karṇa-mala* (*karṇa*/ear, *mala*/dirt/wax). They were Madhu and Kaiṭabha. The demons started attacking Brahmā. Brahmā sought Nārāyaṇa's help. Rousing Nārāyaṇa from his yogic slumber was a hard task, and Śrī Chaṇḍī's help was needed. Eventually Nārāyaṇa woke up and, after a long fight, killed the demons. The fatty substance (*meda*) that oozed out of the huge corpses solidified in the vast expanse of the primordial fluid to form the earth. That is why one of the names of the earth is *medinī* (from *meda*).

In the Vedas, there appears a much more sophisticated form of myth. Underneath the superficial external account, there is a symbolism which adds a new dimension to the myth. Frequent references are made to a war between Indra (leader of gods/*suras*/*devas*) and Vṛtra (leader of demons/*asuras*/*dānavas*). On the surface the story is of a war between the gods and the demons. *Ṛg-veda* (X 147: 1 and II 12: 3) praises Indra, who killed Vṛtra and slit open his belly and consequently let loose the seven torrential streams. Laying the great mountain open, Indra set free the floods that were obstructed before. This 'war episode' turns out to be a creation myth. It has been interpreted as the struggle between the forces of chaos, disorder and inertia on one side, and those of harmony, order and progress on the other. *Sura* means concord and *asura* means discord. *Vṛtra* means darkness. The killing of Vṛtra symbolises the uncovering of darkness and inertia. As a result, streams of light and progress are freed and bring order in place of the chaos that prevailed prior to the creation. The torrential streams represent the primordial fluid out of which the creation materialised. Clearly, Indra is the creator according to this myth.

There are other myths where the credit of creation goes to other deities. One such deity is Prajāpati, meaning the Lord (*pati*) of the people/creatures (*prajā*). From within the belly of Prajāpati emerged the primordial fluid, out of which the creation materialised. Then there is Viśvakarman (*viśva*/all/world, *karman*/maker) whose very name proclaims him as the maker of all or the architect of the world.

Next came the early metaphysical period, reflected in portions of the Vedas and some other writings. The idea of the uniqueness of a Supreme Creator evolved during this period. The singularity behind the superficial pluralism has been expressed in several hymns (e.g., *Ṛg-veda* VIII 58: 2 and *Yajur-veda* 32: 1), as in the following:

> They speak of Indra, Mitra, Varuṇa, Agni,
> and there is the Divine, winged Suparṇa.
> The One Being the wise call by many names
> as Agni, Yama, Mātariśvan.
>
> (*Ṛg-veda* I 164: 46 and *Atharva-veda* IX 10: 28)

A different class of thinkers emerged in the field of cosmogony, who might be called 'theologian naturalists', as Bhattacharjee (1978: 63) puts it. They were mystified by the unfathomable nature of this universe. The puzzled state of their analytical mind is apparent from the hymn which is hailed as the Hymn of Creation (*Nāsadīya Sūkta*). According to Macdonell (1972: 207), in this 'cosmogonic poem the origin of the world is explained as the evolution of the existent (sat) from the non-existent (asat). Water thus came into being first; from it was evolved intelligence by heat. It is the starting-point of the natural philosophy which developed into the Sāṃkhya system'. (This is explained on p. 58.) The frequent use of questions in the composition of the hymn itself emphasises the unresolved nature of the thinker's quest.

> There was neither the non-existent nor the existent then. There was no air nor the heavens beyond it. What lay covered and where? In whose protection? Was there then the unfathomable cosmic water? There was neither death nor immortality then. There was no sign of night nor of day. The One breathed, windless, by self-impulse. Other than that there was nothing beyond.
>
> At first there was darkness and all this was undistinguishable water. That One arose at last, born of the power of heat (*tapas*). In the beginning desire (*kāma*) came upon it. It was the primal seed, born of the mind. The sages, in their wisdom, discovered the bond of the existent in the non-existent.
>
> Who knows truly? Who can declare? When and how did this creation happen? He, the surveyor of the highest heaven, surely knows; or may be even He does not!
>
> (*Ṛg-veda* X 129: 1–7)

Two important ideas appear in this hymn: the role of desire (*kāma*) as the first initiating factor, and the part played by heat (*tapas*) in materialising the creative process. In addition, 'the symbol of water is the most pertinent one: the primordial water covers all, . . . it is the first condition of life, the place of the original seed, the fertilizing milieu' (Panikkar 1979: 56).

But the climax of the *Ṛg-veda* in the field of cosmogony is considered to be the concept of *hiraṇya-garbha*, which was widely accepted and elaborated by later thinkers in subsequent works: the *Brāhmaṇas*, the *Upaniṣads* and the *Purāṇas*. The term (*hiraṇya*/gold, *garbha*/womb) stands for an object whose interior is extremely bright. According to the hymn, *Hiraṇya-Garbha* (*Ṛg-veda* X 121), and other sources, the first creation appeared out of primordial fluid as an object with an extremely bright interior, and from it the present form of the universe evolved in stages.

The *Brāhmaṇas* also have passages on the creation process. The creation of *mahābhūtas* (the fundamental physical elements, namely, earth, water, heat, air and space) has been described in some. The *Aitareya Brāhmaṇa* (V 32) suggests a picture of successive creation of the gross elements.

In the upanisadic stage, again several points of development emerged. The *Muṇḍaka Upaniṣad* (I 1: 7–8) says:

> As the web comes out of the spider and is withdrawn, as plants grow from the soil and hairs from the body of man, so springs the universe from [within] the Eternal.
>
> With the will to multiply Brahman [the Supreme Being] expanded and then came the primeval matter out of him. From this came the primal energy. From that came mind, from mind the subtle elements, from elements the many worlds.

Six systems of philosophy (*darśana*)

Following the theologian naturalists, there appeared a class of rationalist thinkers or philosophers in the proper sense. They attacked the whole riddle of cosmology with a new type of precision in methodology, introducing intellectual analyses of the subject. The diversity of opinion resulted in the development of six main schools. But there is one very basic underlying factor which is common to all these systems, and that is an emphatic declaration that their aim is not to pursue knowledge for knowledge's sake, but to find a way of eliminating suffering,[3] or to find the cause of suffering in human life and to eliminate the causative factor.

The six main schools of philosophy can be put into three groups according to the individual cosmological theories they follow.

• Nyāya	• Sāṃkhya	• Mīmāṃsā
• Vaiśeṣika	• Yoga	• Vedānta

Three of these schools have distinctive theories of creation:

Vaiśeṣika, Sāṃkhya and Vedānta.

VAIŚEṢIKA

Vaiśeṣika claims that all material objects are made of atoms (*paramāṇus*). Different combinations of atoms with special qualities make up different materials. There are four such special qualities:

- odour (*gandha*)
- taste/flavour (*rasa*)
- form/appearance (*rūpa*)
- touch/feel (*sparśa*).

A combination of all four qualities makes up earth, i.e., all earthy objects have some kind of odour, taste, appearance and are tangible. Water has three special qualities: taste, appearance and touch/feel. Fire has two qualities: appearance and touch/feel. Air has only one: touch/feel.

The Vaiśeṣika school accepts a personal God (*Īśvara*) who created the world, but not out of nothing. The elements existed before the world was formed. He fashioned them into an ordered universe. *Īśvara* is thus the creator of the world, but not of its constituents.

SĀṂKHYA

This school of philosophy deals prominently with the creation of the material universe. It holds that to know an object fully one has to know all of its components. The system is dualistic, recognising two basic principles of creation: *puruṣa* (the male principle) and *prakṛti* (the female principle).

Prakṛti is the primal substance or matter out of which the entire creation evolves. Its constituents are the three *guṇa*s (properties/attributes): *sattva* (purity/harmony), *rajas* (passion/energy) and *tamas* (inertia/darkness). These three *guṇa*s are responsible for all change, and form the basis of evolution. But *prakṛti* lies dormant when its three *guṇa*s are in equilibrium. While *prakṛti* has the potential of creating and destroying the universe by itself, without *puruṣa*'s initiation the process of creation cannot start. As opposed to *prakṛti*, *puruṣa* is *nirguṇa* (without any *guṇa*/attribute) and does not change. As soon as *prakṛti* is united with *puruṣa*, the equilibrium of the *guṇa*s is broken. The agitation of the three *guṇa*s starts the creative process. Through several stages of creation finally appear the five *mahābhūta*s (the fundamental elements):

- *kṣiti* (earth)
- *ap* (water)
- *tejas* (fire/heat)
- *marut*/*vāyu* (air)
- *vyoman* (space).

From the *mahābhūta*s eventually evolves the phenomenal world.

VEDĀNTA (OR UTTARA-MĪMĀṂSĀ)

Vedānta means the 'End of the Vedas' (*anta*/end), i.e., the definitive knowledge of the Vedas. It is also known as Uttara Mīmāṃsā (*uttara*/later; *Mīmāṃsā*/investigation), which means that it is the investigation into the later chapters of the Vedas, that is, the *Upaniṣads*.

From a cosmic standpoint, Vedānta explains the relationship of *Brahman*, the unmanifested Absolute Reality, with the manifested creation by introducing the principle of *māyā*. *Māyā* means illusion – that which is not real but which appears to be real. According to Vedānta, only *Brahman* is real, and the phenomenal world is unreal (*māyā*), and beings are no different from *Brahman*. As Bhattacharjee (1978: 69) points out, it is a bold antithesis of all creation hypotheses. If the phenomenal world is illusory, there need not be any creative process. This world is only an apparent transmutation of *Brahman*. Under the influence of *māyā* this material world appears to be real, but, with true knowledge and diligent investigations, one can see through the unreal world and find *Brahman* in everything.

All the *Upaniṣads* agree that *Brahman*, the ultimate unchanging reality, lies behind this constantly changing (therefore unreal/*māyā*) material world. Regarding the nature of this Absolute Reality (also known as *ātman*/self), the *Upaniṣads* are quite specific. The *Kaṭha Upaniṣad* (I 2: 20) says, 'It is smaller than the smallest and greater than the greatest'. The *Śvetāśvatara Upaniṣad* (V 9) says, 'If the tip of a hair is split a hundred times and that fine part again split a hundred times, then that equals the Self and that is at the same time infinitely extended'.

Brahmāṇḍa

This is a term frequently used in Hindu cosmology. It means the universe in general. Etymologically it means the Egg of Brahman (*aṇḍa*/egg). Both vedic (the *Brāhmaṇas*, the *Upaniṣads*) and non-vedic (the *Purāṇas*) sources give vivid descriptions of this egg. The *Chhāndogya Upaniṣad* (III 19: 1–2) says:

> The non-existent became existent in the form of an egg. Then it lay motionless for a year. Then it got divided. One part of the egg was silvery and the other golden. The silvery one became the earth and the golden one the heaven.

The *Viṣṇu Purāṇa* (I 2: 51) and the *Kūrma Purāṇa* (I 4: 36) say:

> Gradually that material-egg expanded like a water bubble. The unmanifested Viṣṇu made himself manifested and rested in the egg as Brahman.

Two striking points emerge from these two quotations. The first hints at the fragmentation of the original body, and the second supports the theory of the expanding nature of the material-egg (or the universe) as suggested by the *Upaniṣads* (e.g., the *Muṇḍaka Upaniṣad*) at an earlier period.

There are passages in the *Purāṇa*s which indicate that a very large number of *brahmāṇḍa*s are in existence. The *Kūrma Purāṇa*(II 6) says:

> The innumerable brahmāṇḍas of the past, the present brahmāṇḍas made up of the combination of all material elements, and the future brahmāṇḍas whose elements are resting in spirit [soul] level are all dependent on Īśvara's [God's] will/command.

In the same *Purāṇa*, mention has been made of fourteen types of *brahmāṇḍa*s (I 44: 1).

The term *brahmāṇḍa*, in these cases, may be compared with galaxies. It is not just one *brahmāṇḍa* that was created, once, a very long time ago, and that we know here and now, but it is a continuous process of creation and dissolution of *brahmāṇḍa*s throughout eternity.

The Hindu scholars had clear concepts about the position of the earth in the universe and its relation with the other stellar bodies. Ārya Bhaṭṭa (fifth century) wrote: 'The stars in the firmament and the sun are static, it is the earth that by its own rotation is causing either the rising or the setting of the planets and stars' (quoted by Bhattacharjee 1978: 6).

Theory of evolution

The Hindu treatises that deal with creation, evolution and dissolution are called the *Purāṇa*s. The term *purāṇa* (*purā*/ancient) signifies 'dealing with ancient topics'. It is the *Purāṇa*s that claim for the first time that the process of creation and evolution is a purely physical one. The *Viṣṇu Purāṇa* (I 4: 52) says:

> The matter [the universal stuff] evolves into the material form by virtue of its own potentialities and that requires no other agency to effect the transformation.

Regarding evolution, both the *Viṣṇu Purāṇa* (I 5: 18–23) and the *Agni Purāṇa* (XX 1–6) say that there are several stages (*sarga*s), and that the highest form of evolution is yet to come.

1. *Mahat sarga* – the creation of infra-physical entities.
2. *Bhūta sarga* – the creation of the fundamental physical elements, namely, earth, water, fire, air and space.
3. *Vaikārika sarga* – the formation of the stellar bodies from the fundamental elements.
4. *Mukhya sarga* – during this stage the inanimate creation (mountains, etc.) was complete.
5. *Tiryak-srotā sarga* – the creation of the first living things that are mobile and grow as a result of taking food, but have no thinking ability or motivation.
6. *Ūrdhva-srotā* (or *Deva*) *sarga* – the creation of deities who are givers of happiness and love.
7. *Arvāk-srotā sarga* – the creation of human beings.
8. *Anugraha sarga* – subdivision of humans into two groups: motivated and positive (because of *sattva guṇa*); and ignorant and negative (because of *tamas guṇa*).
9. *Kaumāra sarga* – the period of evolution of 'supermen' (like Sanat-kumāra, one of the sons of Brahmā).

Apart from this complete theory of evolution, comprising both inanimate and animate creation, there is a myth prevalent in Hindu literature which needs to be mentioned here since it describes, through its narrative, the successive appearance of higher forms of life on this planet. It is the story of the ten *avatāra*s (*daśāvatāra* – *daśa*/ten; *avatāra*/incarnation) or incarnations of Viṣṇu. According to Hindu ideas, God is not different from the created objects. The phenomenal world forms part of the Supreme Being. In times of need, to restore balance or to regain harmony of the world, God manifests himself in the form of a created being. The story is found in several scriptures, and all ten *avatāra*s were recognised by about the eleventh century CE. According to Jayadeva's *Gīta-Govinda* (I 5–14), Lord Viṣṇu saved the earth repeatedly from its predicament.

The narrative, as rendered by Bhattacharjee (1978: 29), starts with the early condition when the surface of the earth was covered with water. In the watery environment, there appeared the first *avatāra*, in the form of a fish (*mīna*/*matsya*). Next, as the water level receded, the second *avatāra* appeared, in the form of a tortoise (*kūrma*). This marks the amphibian stage. This was followed by the appearance of a boar (*varāha*), a pure mammal. The next *avatāra* appeared in the form of a lion-man (*narṣiṃha*), a form intermediate between animal and human. Then came a dwarf (*vāmana*), a short-statured man. The next *avatāra* was Paraśurāma or Rāma with the axe (*paraśu*), a fierce warrior-like character, fully human in form but not humane in nature yet. His warring missions and the murdering of his own mother hint at the brutality of his nature. Then came Rāma, the hero of the epic, *Rāmāyaṇa*. He belonged to the *kṣatriya* (warrior) caste, showing that fighting was a way of life for him. Next was Balarāma, the bearer of the ploughshare (*haladhara*), signifying the settled agricultural phase of society. In a variant form, Kṛṣṇa (the deliverer of the *Bhagavadgītā* in the epic *Mahābhārata*), the younger brother of Balarāma, is the eighth *avatāra*, not Balarāma. The ninth *avatāra* was the Buddha who preached non-violence. The whole evolution from the first aquatic life to the extremely human compassionate Buddha is symbolically expressed here. The tenth *avatāra*, called *Kalkin*, is yet to come. It is predicted in the narrative that his weapon for destroying evil will be something as fierce as a comet (*dhūmaketu*).

Pralaya

Nature, like living creatures, is subject to decay and destruction. But in Hindu thought there is no ultimate destruction or dissolution. It is a continuous cycle of creation, dissolution and re-creation from the dissolved state. *Pralaya* (or *laya*) is the term used for dissolution in general, but various degrees of dissolution are recognised by Hindu thinkers and are described in great detail in various sources.

We start with the story of the deluge of Manu. Descriptions of it are found in both vedic and non-vedic literature. The basic narrative, found in the *Śatapatha Brāhmaṇa* (I 8: 1, 1–10) and the *Mahābhārata* (*Vana-parva*, 187), runs as follows.

There was an ancient sage named Manu who passed his days in religious pursuits. One day when he was washing himself in the river, a little fish came into his hand. The fish asked the sage to save him from the immediate danger of being devoured by a bigger fish. He explained that in the fish community the law of 'might is right' prevails. So a small fish lives in perpetual danger from a bigger fish. The fish also instructed Manu how to tend him carefully. Manu kept him in a jar of water as instructed. When the fish outgrew the jar he was transferred to a pond and later to the sea. Once saved, the fish warned the sage about an imminent great flood that would wash away the whole creation, and asked him to build a large boat and take seeds of all plants and animals with him in the boat. In time the prediction was fulfilled. The water level rose and rose. The fish towed the boat, and anchored it to a peak of the Himalayas. After the destruction, all was created again from Manu. The term for 'human' is *mānava*, which literally means 'of Manu' – descended from Manu.

The destruction described here is not a full-scale one. Compared with other kinds of *pralaya*s vividly described in various *Purāṇa*s, this is only a mini-*pralaya*. According to the *Kūrma Purāṇa* (II 43), a *pralaya* takes place after a specific length of time called a *kalpa*.[4] When the time arrives, the process starts with a prolonged drought. The fragile beings of the earth decay fast and the seven rays of the sun become intense. The water of reservoirs evaporates and the sun looks like seven suns. Gradually the sun's seven rays become a thousand rays, pouring in all directions. In that intense heat everything melts and becomes a single blazing mass. The whole of it then bursts into a larger flame called *saṃvartaka* which starts consuming the worlds (*loka*s). The magnitude of the catastrophe suggests that it would be an astronomical event.

The description goes on to say that, gradually, large columns of highly electrically charged clouds appear in the empty space. These clouds look white, black, yellow, red, grey and deep blue. The fury of the catastrophe goes on for a long time, then slowly things start to change. From within the smoky clouds appears rain, and the space becomes flooded. From that fluid gradually emerges a new creation.

The whole of this process takes another *kalpa* to complete. Two *kalpa*s make a day and a night of Brahmā. The *kalpa* during which creation takes place is the 'day of Brahmā', and the *kalpa* of dissolution is the night. This cyclic process of dissolution and creation goes on against the backdrop of the eternally flowing *kāla* (time).

In these narratives of *pralaya* there is no mention of the element of degeneration of, or sins perpetrated by, humans. But, during the period of the epic *Mahābhārata*, the idea gained ground that in ancient times there lived on earth an ideal race of humans. It was the age of the great sages. Then gradually there is a progressive deterioration of morality, and a degeneration of human society, that needs to be dealt with. The era is brought to a climax of dissolution by a great deluge, as there was a need for a complete clean-up, so to speak. This deterioration from the ideal to the vile state takes a very long time and happens very gradually, through four stages or eras (*yuga*s): *satya*, *tretā*, *dvāpara* and *kali*.[5] The general concept behind these divisions is that in *Satya yuga*, the whole humanity is truthful and its moral values are intact; in *Tretā yuga*, three quarters of human society are truthful and one quarter degenerate; in *Dvāpara yuga*, only a half are moral; and in *Kali yuga*, only one quarter are truthful. There are specific references to the present era being the *Kali yuga* of the current creation (e.g., in the *Viṣṇu Purāṇa*).

The theory of *daśāvatāra* is based on the same criterion of morality (*dharma*) and right conduct. Lord Kṛṣṇa's utterance in the *Bhagavadgītā* (IV 6–8) makes it clear:

> Though I am unborn and of imperishable nature, though Lord of all beings, yet remaining in my own nature I take birth through my own power of creation. Whenever *dharma* is in decay and *adharma* flourishes, O Bhārata, then I create myself. To protect the righteous and destroy the wicked, to establish *dharma* firmly, I take birth age after age.

The natural environment

To trace the development of the Hindu attitude towards the natural environment, one has to go back to the vedic literature, where the earliest hymns dedicated to the natural elements are found. The powerful forces of nature inspired human awe and bewilderment, and consequently a whole culture grew up glorifying and appeasing them. Natural phenomena were revered, and personified as various deities, for example, the sun, fire, storm, lightning. On the one hand, people were offering oblations and chanting hymns to glorify the deities, and, on the other, they were asking favours from them in return, in the form of a good harvest, cattle, children and well-being in general. Vedic worship seems to have been the performance of sacrifices in the open air, around a fire. Worship in relation to nature was clearly a preoccupation in this period.

The most intimate, beneficent, household deity was Agni (fire). He was considered to be a friend, a father, and a messenger from humans to the other deities in the heavens. The ascending flames and smoke of the sacrificial fire seem to have given him the status of heavenly messenger or mediator. Some two hundred hymns were addressed to Agni. The very first hymn of the *Ṛg-veda*, the central part of the entire vedic revelation, is an invocation to Agni (I 1). Here he is described as the domestic priest (*purohita*), the divine minister (*ṛtvij*) of the sacrifice. He is the mediator who transforms all material and human gifts into spiritual and divine realities, and delivers them to the heavenly deities, bringing back the divine blessings to the human worshippers. Agni has a priestly role and a three-fold composition, his nature being divine, human and earthly at one and the same time.

Reverence is due to Parjanya (rain cloud), Vāyu (wind), Maruts (storm gods), Savitṛ (solar god) and Sūrya (the sun), among many other vedic deities who are in some way or another linked with natural occurrences. Of these, Sūrya is the most concrete of the solar deities – since the name specified the orb of the sun as well as the deity, his connection with the luminary was always present in the mind of the sages.

> The golden gem of the sky, far-seeing rises, whose goal is distant, speeding onward, shining. Now may men, aroused by the Sun, attain their goals and perform their labours.
>
> (*Ṛg-veda* (VII 63: 4), trans. Macdonell 1972: 127)

Vedic people not only composed hymns to glorify the natural phenomena, to appease them or to thank them for their earthly gifts, but also composed pure poetry inspired by the sheer beauty of nature. The hymns to Uṣas (dawn) are among the most beautiful of all hymns of the *Ṛg-veda*. Some twenty hymns are addressed to Uṣas, the Daughter of Heaven, who is born of Dyu (sky). She is the Lady of Light, consort of the Sun, who follows her as a young man follows a maiden (*Ṛg-veda* I 115: 2). The Goddess of Hope, the elder sister of Niśā (night), Uṣas is mentioned more than 300 times in the *Ṛg-veda*.

Besides the natural elements and the heavenly bodies, humans see themselves surrounded by nature near at hand, complete with its plants and animals and other, apparently inanimate, objects. They feel akin to this environment, so much so that they develop an animistic view of nature, believing that there is life or soul in every little thing in nature. Even apparently inanimate rivers and mountains are believed to have some kind of hidden consciousness, according to the *Kālikā Purāṇa* (22: 10–13), just as a shell seems lifeless but contains a living being inside. Humans see themselves not as isolated beings but as a constituted relationship, incorporated with the rest of the living community. The following hymn from the *Ṛg-veda* (I 90: 6–8), known as the *Madhumatī Sūkta*, shows how vedic people recognised and appreciated nature's beneficence.

> For one who lives by Eternal Law [*ṛta*]
> the winds are full of sweetness;
> the rivers pour sweets;
> so may plants be full of sweetness for us.
> Sweet be the night and sweet the dawns;
> and sweet the dust of the earth.
> Sweet be our Father Heaven to us.
> For us may the forest tree be full of sweetness,
> full of sweetness the sun,
> and full of sweetness the cows for us.

This may be called vedic 'paganism' – the joy in the earth, but a joy sanctified under the control of Eternal Law (*ṛta*), as Bose (1970: 253) points out. The expression 'Eternal Law' here is significant. *Ṛta* means, on the one hand, the regular order of the universe/nature, such as the unvarying course of the sun and moon, and of the seasons; on the other, the moral order. The hymn then emphasises that only the person who abides by the natural law (i.e., who does not exploit nature) and keeps harmony with nature, may be blessed by all things in nature and make a heaven of the earth. Hence, the human relationship with nature is not one of exploitation but one of harmonious participation. Nature is never left out in human social ceremonies. The final chant or the *śānti-vachana* (words of peace) at the end of all Hindu rituals or celebrations, captures the spirit of the entire natural world:

> Peace of sky, peace of mid-region,
> peace of earth, peace of waters, peace of plants.
> Peace of trees, peace of all gods, peace of Brahman,

peace of the universe, peace of peace,
May that peace come to me.

(*Yajur-veda*, VS 36: 17 and *Atharva-veda*, XIX 9: 94)

From these vedic hymns it is evident that the natural world, with its animate and inanimate components, is not to be ignored by humans; on the contrary, it is welcomed ceremonially at most rituals. The attitude is one of recognition of the fact that humans are only a part of the whole natural world. Hence all should co-exist and complement one another. The destruction of one may put the balance of this whole world into jeopardy.

The reverence for the earth takes literal form in India. The earth is the foundation, the basis from which emerges all that exists and on which everything rests. Not surprisingly, the earth is Mother. She is the basis of life, and, when considered as a divine being, she always occupies a special place among deities. Though only one hymn in the *Ṛg-veda* is addressed to Pṛthivī (earth) specifically, she is praised in several hymns conjointly with Dyu (sky). Dyu and Pṛthivī are called father and mother, not only of terrestrial creatures but of the gods too. Worshipping earth is not idolatry. It is the veneration shown, so to speak, to an ancestor, continuing even today; the simple tradition of Bharatanāṭyam (a classical dance form of South India) – with the dancer's first gesture, of touching the earth and thereby begging forgiveness for treading upon her – reveals this veneration.

One of the most beautiful hymns of the Vedas, the famous prayer to the earth called *Bhūmi Sūkta*, consisting of sixty-three verses, is found in the *Atharva-veda* (XII 1). The earth is here called *bhūmi* (ground/land) and not *pṛthivī* (literally, the broad one). This hymn depicts the universal mother, giver of every sort of good. It presents a striking cosmogonic sequence, as can be seen from Panikkar (1979: 121–22): The description starts with the origin of the earth. She was hidden in the fluid state in the bosom of the primordial waters and the sages were seeking her through meditation. Then comes a geographical description, a highly poetical vision of nature. The earth is composed of hills and plains, of snow-clad peaks, of deserts, oceans and rivers, of lakes and streams, trees and plants, rocks and stones. The seasons appear with unfailing regularity and bring to her their own gradations of climate. Her fragrance emanates from plants, from water, from animals, from humans, even from the gods. She is rich with underground treasures of jewels and gold. Earth is the dwelling place of people. The first humans were scattered upon her, and upon her they sing and dance and find their happiness. It is she who diversifies human speech into different languages. She is the dwelling place of all living creatures. She is the home of lions and tigers, the beasts of the forest, of deer and birds, reptiles and two-legged creatures. Mention is made even of snakes and scorpions that viciously bite and, chilled by winter, lie lazily hidden, and of tiny wriggling worms that stir in the rain. She is, finally, the Mother, a cosmic power, the receiver of prayers and the bestower of blessings, and the protector.

As the human role evolves from being a passive receiver of earth's produce to being an active toiler on the land, the relationship with nature matures into a partnership. Human involvement in the process of producing food is an act of collaboration with the earth/nature – we learn to work with nature. On the other hand, the earth is happy to be worked by those who are helping her to produce more and to reach her own plenitude. It is not a relationship of dominion or of exploitation. A hymn addressed to Kṣetra-pati (lord/*pati*; of the field/*kṣetra*) as a friend, expresses this reliance on the earth as a partner. The reciter of the hymn begs the spirit of the field to watch over the ploughman's toil and to cause the earth to produce bountifully.

> Having the Lord of the Field as our friend and helper, may our cattle and horses have food in plenty. May men and oxen both plough in contentment, in contentment the plough cleave the furrow. Auspicious Furrow, we venerate you. We pray you, bless us and bring us abundant harvests.
>
> (*Ṛg-veda* IV 57)

When the tilling of the soil is over, then comes the prayer for a bountiful harvest (*Atharva-veda* VI 142) and the harvest song (*Atharva-veda* III 24). The last verse of the harvest song, called *Samṛddhi-prāpti*, mentions even reaper and garnerer as the two distributors or attendants of Prajāpati (lord/*pati* of the creatures/*prajā*).

Any civilisation which is mainly dependent on agriculture has a special relationship with its mother earth, who is the eternal provider of food. Timely rain, rivers and tributaries, seasonal changes in nature, are all of primary importance. To an agricultural community, nature is a living reality; at times harsh and cruel, at other times loving and generous. That is why earth is an object of worship and not of exploitation. This is how the Hindus of the past saw nature.

India today is still a country very much dependent on nature. Even in the present age of vast industrialisation and high technology, seventy per cent of its population depend on agriculture. Yet the necessity for economic development has led India to look for desperate measures, at the expense of natural resources that took hundreds of years to establish; the felling of trees is one of them. Unexpected floods, the increase of barren desert areas and environmental changes are all linked with deforestation, and are signs of disharmony with, and exploitation of, nature. The ideals preached by the ancient Hindus are not always followed in actual practice in modern India. But at grass-roots level, a predominantly rural population still looks up to the Mother Earth as the life-sustaining living reality. The 'Chipko' (hug-the-tree) movement, which started in 1974 and spread all over India, proves the point. It is a movement that grew from the simple act of hugging the trees by the village women of Reni in Garhwal, thus stopping the hired workers, who were about to cut down the trees for a sports-goods company.

The plant world

Forests have always played a central part in Hindu civilisation. Forest life is the third of the four *āśrama*s (stages in the life of a high caste Hindu: *brahmacharya*/student life, *gārhasthya*/family life, *vānaprastha*/forest life and *sannyāsa*/ascetic life). The term *vānaprastha* is derived from the word *vana*, meaning woodland. In this third stage, the individual takes leave of society and retires to a forest life for reflection and self-searching. As Jyoti Sahi (1986: 43) points out, 'forest' has a particular symbolic meaning in Hindu thought, rather like the 'wilderness' of Jewish and Christian thought. The forest is seen in contrast with the cultivated land. In a way, the individual must return to the way of life of the pre-agricultural societies, the food-gathering way of the herdsman. It is not that a

Hindu has no experience of a developed urban life (names of very many cities could be cited), but he consciously chooses to model human life in close proximity to nature, where the process of rejuvenation goes on perpetually. According to Rabindranath Tagore, the uniqueness of Hindu ideology consists in recognising life in the forest as the highest form of cultural evolution. He writes (in *Tapovana*, as quoted by Shiva, 1989: 55):

> Indian civilisation has been distinctive in locating its source of regeneration, material and intellectual, in the forest, not in the city. India's best ideas have come where man was in communion with trees and rivers and lakes, away from the crowds. The peace of the forest has helped the intellectual evolution of man. The culture of the forest has fuelled the culture of Indian society. The culture that has arisen from the forest has been influenced by the diverse processes of renewal of life which are always at play in the forest, varying from species to species, from season to season, in sight and sound and smell. The unifying principle of life in diversity, of democratic pluralism, thus became the principle of Indian civilization.

The vedic poet even worships Araṇyānī (Sprite of the Forest/*araṇya*) as a deity. The hymn to Araṇyānī (*Ṛg-veda* X 146: 2,6) shows that the woodland is appreciated not merely for its generous gifts of shelter, food and pure air, but is venerated for its inspiring quality of sight, sound and smell. The hymn is a piece of pure poetry without any motivation attached to it.

> When the cicada emits his shrill notes
>   and the grasshopper is his accompanist,
> it's the Sprite of the Forest they hail with their praises,
>   as with cymbals clashing in procession.
>
> Adorned with fragrant perfumes and balms,
>   she needs not to toil for her food.
> Mother of untamed forest beasts,
>   Sprite of the wood, I salute you!

(Quoted from Panikkar 1979: 276)

Apart from the *Saṃhitā* (hymn) period, there is a whole set of vedic literature called *Āraṇyaka*s (Forest Texts) that contains the knowledge which comes from direct participation in the life of the forest. The forest 'nurtured an ecological civilization in the most fundamental sense of harmony with nature' (Shiva 1989: 56).

In non-vedic literature also, plant life is venerated and associated with divinity, e.g., in *Śrī Chaṇḍī* (a part of the *Mārkaṇḍeya Purāṇa*) (XI 48), the primordial Mother Chaṇḍī proclaims that she nourishes the whole world with the life-sustaining vegetation that grows out of her own body.

The Hindu ideal of elevating plant life to the level of divinity is evident from the common practice of tree or plant worship in India. There are certain trees or plants that are considered sacred for various reasons. For example, the banyan tree is considered to have a benign effect on people searching for spiritual enlightenment. The Buddha, believed by Hindus to be the ninth incarnation of Viṣṇu, achieved his enlightenment meditating under a type of banyan tree called *aśvattha* (ficus religiosa), subsequently known as the *bodhi* Tree (tree of knowledge) in the city of Bodh Gaya. The nineteenth century saint, Ramakrishna, achieved his vision under another type of banyan tree, called *vaṭa* (ficus benghalensis) in Dakshineswar in Bengal.

The daily worship of the sacred plant *tulasī* (ocymum sanctum) is prevalent all over India. It is a little herbal plant which has medicinal value and is used in herbal (Āyurvedic) treatments. But besides its beneficial properties, it has a religious significance for its devotees. It is a symbol of Lord Viṣṇu. Women, when they water the *tulasī* every morning and light a lamp at its altar in the evening, do not think of it as a mere plant, but are filled with veneration and humility, as in the presence of a deity. In the form of a small plant, nature is elevated to divinity.

Similarly, other trees, plants and flowers are associated with particular deities. *Bilva* (crataeva religiosa), *javā* (hibiscus) and *kamala* (nymphaea lotus) are associated with Śiva, Kālī/Durgā and Lakṣmī respectively. There are even special dates in the Hindu calendar for the worship of particular plants.

ĀYURVEDA (LIFE-SCIENCE)

People in the vedic period recognised their indebtedness to the plant world for an additional reason. The medical science based on the knowledge of herbs and plants is called Āyurveda (*āyur*/life, *veda*/

knowledge). It is often known as the fifth Veda or an *upaveda* (or a part or sub-group) of *Atharva-veda*, showing the high regard it attracted as a life-science. Herbal medicine flourished in India for centuries. Even in today's India there is a large number of followers of Āyurveda, which in the West is considered to be one of the alternative medicines. The main basis of Āyurveda lies in the concept of balance of elements in the human body. Like any material body, the human body is made up of five elements: earth (*kṣiti*), water (*ap*), heat (*tejas*), air (*marut/vāyu*) and space (*vyoman*). When all these elements in their particular proportions are working in proper balance, the body is fit. When somehow these respective proportions go wrong and the balance is not perfect, the body becomes ill. The Āyurveda prescribes various plants and roots for rectifying different kinds of imbalance.

There are hymns in the *Atharva-veda* (e.g., IV 17) addressed to plants for their power of curing particular diseases, thus acknowledging humanity's indebtedness to the plant world for its contribution towards human welfare.

From a study of Āyurveda one can see how detailed was the vedic knowledge of medicinal properties of herbs, and how delicately medicine was administered in each individual case. The *Atharva-veda* mentions about 110 plants used in the cure of various ailments, and most of these remedies did come to occupy a significant place in the ayurvedic literature of later periods. In the *Ṛg-veda* also, there is a hymn addressed to *Oṣadhi* (herbal plant) (X 97) which mentions several herbs, and distinguishes between herbs bearing flowers and fruits and herbs without them. Vegetation itself is divided into various categories, e.g., *vanaspati* is the forest tree that bears fruit without any blossom, or *oṣadhi* is the annual plant that dies after the ripening of fruits.

That the Hindus had a detailed knowledge of various species of trees and plants is also evident from terms like *vanaspati-vidyā* (*vidyā*/knowledge/science) meaning tree-science; and terms like *vṛkṣāyurveda* (*vṛkṣa*/tree, *āyurveda*/life-science), meaning the science of treatment of trees, show that treatments for trees were practised.

The animal world

While the Aryan deities were mostly personifications of natural phenomena or heavenly bodies, the indigenous non-Aryan peoples had rituals of image worship of male and female deities. Several mystic animals had their place in the rituals too. Various animals or birds are associated with particular deities as their vehicles (*vāhana*) and companions. One deity (Kārtikeya – male) is mounted on the peacock, another (Sarasvatī – female) on the swan, a third (Śiva – male) is carried by the bull, a fourth (Durgā – female) by the lion, and so on. Because of their association with the deities, these animals and birds are considered sacred. Apart from the peacock, swan, bull and lion, others belonging to this sacred list include goat, buffalo, elephant, tiger, serpent, rat and owl. Together with the deities, the respective animals are worshipped and praised.

The clash of cults (in the present context, Aryan and non-Aryan) or the contacts of cultures do not necessarily result in a complete domination of one by the other. There may be an interchange of concepts, with old concepts being given new significance. There are stories in the Epic literature (the *Rāmāyaṇa*) indicating the reconciliation of the vedic and the non-vedic faiths. As Radhakrishnan (1971: 30) pointed out, 'The enlistment of Hanumān, the monkey-general, in the service of Rāma, signifies the meeting-point of early nature worship and later theism'.

In Hindu mythology, the frequent occurrences of transformations of humans into animals and vice versa show the recognition that animal life is as valid as, and thus interchangeable with, human life. The Hindu theory of transmigration of the soul accepts the logic that a soul taking births into several forms may take animal forms as well as human. Though it may seem strange, this hints at the acceptance of the idea that, in the strata of living creatures, humans are not necessarily put on an unchallenged pedestal. The positions of humans and animals are interchangeable when circumstances demand, or *karma* (consequence of deeds from previous lives) dictates.

In the story of *Daśāvatāra* (ten incarnations), Lord Viṣṇu himself takes several births into animal forms before taking human ones. It is significant that Hindus do not find it hard or unnatural to think of their God in animal forms. On the contrary, they find it most natural and plausible if they are to believe that creation is an evolutionary process, and that life began in its minutest forms. If their God himself can take up the humble forms of a fish (aquatic), a tortoise (amphibian), a boar (terrestrial) and a lion-man (half-human), before human forms, it shows the kind of regard or reverence Hindus feel towards the animal world. This story puts humans in their proper perspective. They are just one of the creatures created during the process of evolution; they owe their existence to their predecessors, the creatures of the animal kingdom.

There are also other areas of human indebtedness to the animal world recognised by the Hindu scriptures. References have been made to animals' knowledge of the medicinal properties of herbs. It is not only humans who have familiarity with the plant world for health and cure; the animals perhaps have a priority over humans in this context. In *Atharva-veda* (VIII 7: 23–4), where various plants are invoked to cure human ailments, mention is made of individual plants being known to boars, hawks, eagles, swans, birds and wild beasts.

In the puranic literature (e.g., in the *Mārkaṇḍeya Purāṇa – Śrī Chaṇḍī* I 49–51), it is recognised that the birds and animals have intelligence of some kind. The difference between the intelligence of animals and the intellect of humans lies in the fact that humans can, if they wish, develop spiritual wisdom beyond the inborn instinctive material sense. To begin with, humans are no wiser than animals. Without the Ultimate Knowledge, humans are equal to animals in intelligence because both are ignorant, knowing merely the sensual world.

The 'holy cow' of the Hindus is a frequently-used phrase in the West. The sanctity of the cow probably has been acquired by its association with Lord Kṛṣṇa, a deity and an incarnation of Viṣṇu. The mythology has it that Kṛṣṇa was brought up as a dairyman's son who used to graze the cattle. The cow is even worshipped in some parts of India on an auspicious day called *Goṣṭhāṣṭamī* in the month of Kārtika (in November), a special day set aside for the cow. 'Whatever origin or value we may ascribe to the sanctity and worship of the cow in India, the fact remains that for a predominantly agricultural civilization the worth of the cow cannot easily be over estimated' (Panikkar 1979: 286). The herd of cattle is an asset to the farmer. The oxen are used for ploughing, the cows produce milk from which come all kinds of dairy products. Cows are not only the source of almost inexhaustible riches, they also symbolise maternity, endurance and service. It is common knowledge that a Hindu does not eat beef. The ban on the slaughtering of cows involves not only religious but also economic factors in an agricultural Hindu society.

VEGETARIANISM

The Aryans enjoyed the meat of sacrificial animals. There are references which show that, in vedic culture, great honour was shown to a guest by offering young calf's meat for his meal (e.g., the sage Vaśiṣṭha was served with veal in the hermitage of the sage Vālmīki – Uttara-Rāmacharita), though they seem to have admired the cow as a very useful animal. The ideals of vegetarianism and non-violence (*ahiṃsā*) developed under the influence of Buddhism and Jainism, and flourished in the sixth century BCE, though the first seeds of non-violence were sown in the *Upaniṣads*. The upanisadic concept of all living creatures being part and parcel of *Brahman* emphasises the sacredness of all forms of life, and thus the killing of animals is unjustifiable. During the developing period of Buddhism and Jainism – two contemporaneous ideologies – this moral issue gained ground. Gradually they evolved into two similar but distinct faiths. As Sen (1973: 64) pointed out, the vedic interest in gods had by then been replaced by interest in humanity and in human greatness. The vedic ideal of a pleasant life on earth had been challenged by believers in renunciation, ego-lessness and selfless work. Jainism contributed to Hindu thought and practices to a great extent, and the vegetarianism of some sects of Hindus may be due to Jain influence. A strong sense of love and compassion for animals and other sub-human species led to vegetarianism. One must remember though, in this context, that not all Hindus are vegetarians, e.g., Bengalis are non-vegetarians. That vegetarianism was widespread in India from a very early period is known from the accounts of the ancient Greek traveller, Megasthenes (fourth century BCE), and those of Fa-hsien (fifth century CE), a Chinese Buddhist monk who travelled to India to obtain authentic copies of the Buddhist scriptures.

The fact that the animals were treated compassionately in Hindu society is documented by the sixteenth-century English traveller, Ralph Fitch, who came across a veterinary hospital in Cooch Bihar. As quoted by Sen (1973: 25):

> I went from Bengala into the country of Couche. Here they be all gentiles and they will kill nothing. They have hospitals for sheepe, goates, dogs, cats, birds, and for all other living creatures. When they be old and lame, they keep them until they die. If a man catch or buy any quicke thing in

other places and bring it thither, they will give him money for it or other victuals, and keepe it in their hospitals or let it go.

(*Early Travels in India* (1921) William Foster (ed.) Oxford University Press, pp. 24–5)

This shows that social or public service was not restricted to humans, but was extended to other living creatures. The continuation of the same trend can be noticed in the preachings of Swami Vivekananda, the Hindu visionary and social reformer, at the turn of the nineteenth century (1863–1902):

Where do you seek your God,
overlooking Him in various forms, in front of you?
He serves God best,
who is kind to all His creatures.

NOTES

1. The term *Hindu* is not of Indian origin. It was given to the people of India by the various invaders who entered India through the mountain passes in the north-west. The first Indians they encountered lived by the River Sindhu (the Indus). *Sindhu* became *Hindu* to the Persians as 's' was replaced by 'h' in their language. Later on the Greeks changed *Hindu* to *Indus* due to the absence of an 'h' sound in theirs. The river *Indus* gave *India* its westernised name. The Indians themselves call their motherland *Bhārata* (the land of Bharata, an ancient king). The term *Hindu* never occurs in ancient Indian literature. It has a geographical rather than a religious connotation.
2. The *Purāṇa*s are the bulk of literature dealing with ancient (*purā*) accounts. They are not directly based on the Vedas, but accept their authority. There are eighteen *Purāṇa*s in all.
3. There are three types of suffering:
   (a) *Ādhyātmika* – mental or spiritual suffering rooted in the soul (*ātman*).
   (b) *Ādhibhautika* – physical suffering caused by imbalance of material elements (*bhūta*) in the body.
   (c) *Ādhidaivika* – accidental suffering caused by fate (*daiva*).
4. A *kalpa* is a specific period of time described in the *Purāṇa*s: 1 *kalpa* = 4,000 *yuga*s or 1,000 *mahāyuga*s (great *yuga*s), since 4 *yuga*s = 1 *mahāyuga*. 1 *mahāyuga* = 4,320,000 human years, therefore 1 *kalpa* = 4,320,000,000 years.

5. The four *yugas* each have a specific duration according to the *Purāṇas*:
   (i) *Satya yuga* = 1,728,000 years
   (ii) *Tretā yuga* = 1,296,000 years
   (iii) *Dvāpara yuga* = 864,000 years
   (iv) *Kali yuga* = 432,000 years.

FURTHER READING

Bhattacharjee, S. (1978) *The Hindu Theory of Cosmology*, Calcutta, Bani Prakashani.

Bose, A.C. (1970) *The Call of the Vedas* (3rd edn), Bombay, Bharatiya Vidya Bhavan.

Macdonell, A.A. (1972) *A Vedic Reader for Students* (3rd edn), London, Oxford University Press.

Panikkar, R. (1979) *The Vedic Experience – Mantramañjarī: An Anthology of the Vedas for Modern Man and Contemporary Celebration* (2nd edn), London, Darton, Longman & Todd.

Radhakrishnan, (1971) *The Hindu View of Life* (16th edn), London, Unwin Books.

Sahi, J. (1986) *Stepping Stones*, Bangalore, Asian Trading Corporation.

Sen, K.M. (1973) *Hinduism* (8th edn), London, Penguin Books.

Shiva, V. (1989) *Staying Alive: Women, Ecology and Development* (2nd edn), London, Zed Books.

4. Islam

Martin Forward and Mohamed Alam

The message of Islam is primarily addressed to human beings, instructing them how to obey God, communicating to them the joys of complying with his commands, and the penalties of disobedience. All other issues are secondary to God's will for human beings.

Nevertheless, Islam has much to say about how such obedience issues in a just and harmonious relationship between humans and the rest of the natural world. Equally, it warns of the consequences of disobedience in human plunder and exploitation of the planet earth. Although Islam usually describes the created order in terms of its relationship to the needs and destiny of human beings, it also reflects upon aspects of creation for its own sake. Most Muslims have regarded all creation, except for humans, as intrinsically obedient to God – obeying, in its amazing variety, the purposes for which he made it.

Although many Muslims have sympathy for the ecological movements widespread today, their religion grants to nature no eternal and enduring value or existence. The cosmos provides an arena in which God addresses human beings, and a home in which he has temporarily set them. One day, he will bring it to an end. Those humans who have obeyed him will enter Paradise, and others will go to hell. The rest of creation will be destroyed: it will have fulfilled its function as humanity's temporary home.

Sources of guidance

The most authoritative source of guidance for Muslims about any matter, especially of law, dogma or ritual, is their sacred scripture, the Qur'ān. The angel Gabriel (*Jibrā'īl*, in Arabic) revealed it piecemeal and in Arabic to Muhammad,[1] the last of the prophets, at irregular intervals from 610 to 632, the year of his death.[2] Believers hold it to be God's uncreated word, binding upon them and relevant for all humankind.

The next most important source is tradition (in Arabic *ḥadīth*). In Islam, this has the specialist sense of being a record of the sayings and doings of Muhammad, witnessed by his earliest companions. As such, it is second in importance only to the Qur'ān itself as a source of guidance for Muslims. There are many compilations of the traditions. Muslims treat six with especial respect, and, of these, two are particularly famous: those of Muhammad b. Isma'il al-Bukhari (810–70) and Abu 'l-Husayn Muslim b. al-Hajjaj (817–75). These two collections together are called 'The Two *Ṣaḥīḥ*s'. *Ṣaḥīḥ* (meaning sound) is a technical term in *ḥadīth* criticism, indicating the highest level of trustworthiness in a tradition. A less satisfactory and much later collection than those of the six is the *Mishkāt al-Māṣabīḥ*, originally put together in the twelfth century by Imam Husayn al-Baghawi. Two centuries later, it was revised by Shaikh Wali al-Din, who gave it its present title, which means 'niche for lamps'. In the South Asian subcontinent, it is widely used among Sunni Muslims (those who follow the *sunnah*, or 'manner of life' of Muhammad, recorded in the traditions and developed Muslim law – about ninety per cent of all Muslims), so we have included some of the traditions it records.

On the basis of the Qur'ān and upon tradition, scholars of jurisprudence assembled and codified the law.[3] We shall, therefore, record some of the sayings of eminent Muslim jurists, scholars who have interpreted Islamic law.

God and his creation

The Qur'ān reveals that the universe came into being by command of the one God: 'Verily, when He intends a thing, His command is, "Be", and it is!' (*Surāh* 36: 82, cf. 2: 117; 3: 47,59; 6: 73; 16: 40; 19: 35; 40: 68).[4] The term *allāh* is formed from *al-ilāh*, which means 'the One'. It is found over 2500 times in the Qur'ān. God is *the* one – there is no second or third; nothing can be compared to him.

Indeed, it is impossible to render the Arabic *al-ilāh* in a plural form. The Qur'ān stands out strongly against polytheism (6: 22 f.) and Christian trinitarianism (5: 76), because they are interpreted as contradicting its basic teaching that God is the sole creator and lord. The *shahādah*, or confession of faith, which distinguishes a Muslim from others, is, in English: 'There is no god but God, and Muhammad is his prophet'. Muhammad is reported to have said:

> If anyone says a hundred times in a day, 'There is no god but God alone who has not partner, to whom dominion belongs, to whom praise is due, who is omnipotent', he will have a reward equivalent to that for emancipating ten slaves, a hundred blessings recorded for him, a hundred evil deeds obliterated from him; it will be a protection for him from the devil all that day until evening, and no one will bring anything more excellent than he brings, except a man who has done more than he has.
>
> (Robson, 1970, vol. 1: 487)

Therefore, Islam does not teach that creation happened by chance. Nor does it accept that it was formed by many gods; the one God, who alone has been from eternity, and who alone is worthy of praise, brought it into being. Nor does it consider that all things are part of one reality: there is a vast gulf between creator and created, between God and what he has made.

The Qur'ān affirms that God cares for what he has made. He has not generated all things only to leave them alone, indifferent to what happens to them. Although God's nature is not the Qur'ān's primary concern, it is an important secondary one. Every *surāh* except for one (number 9, which may originally have been attached to the previous *surāh*) begins with a description of God as *al-raḥmān al-raḥīm*, 'Most gracious, most merciful'. Moreover, both Bukhari (Khan 1984, vol. 4, no. 416) and Muslim (Siddiqi 1977, vol. 4, no. 6626) record a tradition that Muhammad said 'When Allāh completed the creation, He wrote in His Book which is with Him on His Throne, "My Mercy overpowers My Anger"'.

Primarily, the Muslims' scripture is 'guidance for humankind' (*hudan lil-nāṣ*, 2: 185 and many other places). It is directed to human beings, so that they can obey God's will. Very often, something from God's creation is used to highlight the qualities of the Qur'ān. There is, for example, a tradition, recorded by a number of his companions, that the Prophet said:

> A believer who recites the Qur'ān is like a citron whose fragrance is sweet and whose taste is sweet, a believer who does not recite the Qur'ān is like a date which has no fragrance but has a sweet taste, a hypocrite who does not recite the Qur'ān is like the colocynth which has no fragrance and has a bitter taste, and a hypocrite who recites the Qur'ān is like basil whose fragrance is sweet but whose taste is bitter.
>
> (Robson 1970, vol. 1, no. 447; and Khan 1984, vol. 6, no. 538)

There is little qur'ānic cosmogony, since scripture is not a handbook about speculative scientific philosophies, but rather God's guidance to human beings. Such theories about the cosmos as the Qur'ān contains serve mainly to describe the environment in which humans exist and are addressed by God, or else their dignity as the last-made of all things. Creation took six days, after which God firmly established himself on the 'Throne' (7: 54, 10: 3 etc.). Within this six-day period, God made the earth in two days, and the seven heavens in two days. The mountains were put in place in four days (41: 9–12). Many of the early commentators argue that the first two days of the setting down of the mountains were when God created the earth. Thus they contained creation within six days (Yusuf Ali 1975, n. 4470). A tradition records that the Prophet said:

> Allāh, the Exalted and Glorious, created the clay on Saturday and he created the mountains on Sunday and He created the Trees on Monday and He created the things entailing labour on Tuesday and created light on Wednesday and He caused the animals to spread on Thursday and created Adam (peace be upon him) after *'Aṣr* [the afternoon prayer; the third of the five prescribed daily prayers] on Friday; the last creation at the last hour of the hours of Friday, i.e. between afternoon and night.
>
> (Muslim; in Siddiqi 1977, vol. 4, no. 6707)

Time and numbers are often used figuratively in the Qur'ān, which itself admits that some of its verses are allegorical, and warns its readers against following them to the detriment of those verses that are basic or fundamental (3: 7). The Qur'ān speaks of the creation of seven earths (as well as seven heavens), but according to

Yusuf Ali this alludes to the geological strata of this one earth that human beings inhabit (65: 12; and 1975, n. 5527). He also contends that 'days' 'refers to stages in the evolution of physical nature' (1975, n. 4477), so should not be pressed to a literal meaning.

From the throne, God rules the world, sending down angels, especially Jibrā'īl, with messages (97: 4). Yusuf Ali's judgement (1975, n. 1032) is that the throne is probably a metaphor symbolising authority, power and vigilance. God alone is eternal. No other gods exist. All things die except for him: 'There is no god but He. Everything [that exists] will perish except his own Face. To Him belongs the Command, and to Him will ye [all] be brought back' (28: 88).

All living things are made from water (21: 30), including human beings (25: 54) who are also said to be created from dust and from a sperm-drop (35: 11). There is no contradiction here: dust symbolises the lowliness and creatureliness of humans, whereas water is the basis of all life, and male sperm is the source of human life. Within this universe, all created things play the role God has ordained for them. They are quite literally '*muslim*' (submitters to God) by virtue of fulfilling their appointed roles: 'all creatures in the heavens and on earth [except humans] have, willing or unwilling, bowed to His Will [accepted Islam], and to Him shall they all be brought back' (3: 83). Many Muslim scholars have elaborated this idea, including Abul A'la Maudūdi (1904–80), journalist and founder of the *Jamā'at-i Islāmī* (founded in 1941), a small but influential revivalist movement and party based in Pakistan but with branches elsewhere, including Britain:

> There is law and order among all the units that comprise this universe . . . The sun, the moon, the stars and in fact all the heavenly beings are knit together in a splendid system. They follow an unalterable law and do not make even the slightest deviation from their ordained course . . . As the entire creation obeys the laws of God, the whole universe, therefore, literally follows the religion of Islam – for Islam signifies nothing but obedience and submission to Allāh, the Lord of the universe. The sun, the moon, the earth, and all other heavenly bodies are thus 'Muslim'. So is the case with air, water, and heat, stones, trees and animals. Everything in the universe is 'Muslim' for it obeys God by submission to His laws.[5]

Human beings form the only exception to this rule. In so far as we are born and die within the will of God, we are naturally '*muslim*'. However, the Qur'ān frequently complains that human beings forget God, and need to remember him and his mercies: 'Don't you see that everything in the heavens and earth bows to God in worship – sun, moon, stars, hills, trees, animals, and many people? However, many humans do not, and deserve punishment' (22: 18).

The created universe provides evidence of the fact that we ignore God at our peril.

> Behold! In the creation of the heavens and the earth, and the alternation of night and day – there are indeed signs for men of understanding – Men who celebrate the praises of God, standing, sitting, and lying down on their sides, and contemplate the [wonders of] creation in the heavens and the earth, [with the thought]: 'Our Lord! not for naught hast Thou created [all] this! Glory to Thee! Give us salvation from the Penalty of the Fire'.
>
> (3: 190–1)

The prayerful attitude called for in this passage illustrates the seriousness of the choice that faces human beings. They can either obey God and hope for heaven, or disobey him and go to hell. This choice must not be played down or trivialised. The Qur'ān warns: 'We [God] did not create the heavens and the earth and all that is between them as a sport' (21: 16).

It is possible to ask sceptical questions, but they are not profitable. The Prophet is believed to have said: 'Men will continue to question one another till this is propounded: Allāh created all things but who created Allāh? He who found himself confronted with such a question should say: I affirm my faith in Allāh' (Muslim, in Siddiqi 1977, vol. 3, no. 243).

To some extent, such scepticism can be answered by reflecting upon the clues creation gives about its maker. Our lived and experienced environment provides many clues to God's presence. He can be discerned not only in the movements of the heavenly bodies, but also in the creation of human beings from sperm, in the mystery of death, and in water and fire and other works of nature (56: 57–74). Those who see God through his signs are urged: 'Then celebrate with praises the name of thy Lord, the Supreme!' (56: 74).

Human beings who do not obey God have failed to recognise that creation points beyond itself to God. They see animals, trees, the mountains, the sexual act and all of God's creation as ends in themselves, not signs which disclose his will:

> And they say: 'What is there but our life in this world? We shall die and we shall live, and nothing but Time can destroy us.' But of that they have no knowledge: they merely conjecture.
>
> (45: 24)

Such cynics do not realise that God will call them to account on the Last Day. There is no reason for their scepticism, because creation is alive with signs of God's presence:

> Do they not look at the sky above them? – How We have made it and adorned it, and there are no flaws in it? And the earth – We have spread it out, and set thereon mountains standing firm, and produced therein every kind of beautiful growth [in pairs] – to be observed and commemorated by every devotee turning [to God]. And We send down from the sky rain charged with blessing, and We produce thee with Gardens and Grain for harvests; And tall [and stately] palmtrees, with shoots of fruit-stalks, piled one over another, – as sustenance for [God's] Servants; – and We give [new] life therewith to land that is dead: thus will be the Resurrection.
>
> (50: 6–11)

However, the natural world and, indeed, the whole cosmos, provide an indirect way of perceiving God's intention for humanity: their signs are, to some extent, oblique. There is a more direct method of apprehending God's will, through the revelation of scripture. Some of the prophets who came, from time to time, to human communities brought a scripture. The Qur'ān points to itself as the ultimate and incomparable sign and miracle; 'in it is Mercy and a Reminder to those who believe (29: 51).[6] Indeed, the Qur'ān is the 'clear sign' (15: 1) to humanity of its need to hear and obey God through his words that it contains. Each verse of the Qur'ān is called in Arabic, *āyāh*, or a 'sign' of God – his direct revelation to human beings as opposed to the more ambiguous signs of nature.

The spirit-world

Revelation instructs human beings about supranatural beings, angels and *jinn*. Indeed, without revelation we would not know of them, since they are not part of the world scanned by our senses. Angels (in Arabic, *malā'ikah*) are bodiless beings created from light who, unlike human beings, render absolute praise, service and obedience to God. Everyone has two recording angels who record his or her good and bad deeds (50: 17 f.). They are called *kirāman al-kātibīn*, 'the Noble Writers', and are regularly greeted during prayers when the worshippers move their heads to the right and the left saying, 'Peace be upon you' (*al-sālamu 'alaykum*). Then there are the 'angels of punishment' (*al-zabānīyah*, which literally means, 'those who thrust violently'), nineteen in number, who are the guardians of hell (96: 18; 74: 30).

The *jinn* are another form of creation. They are intelligent, often invisible, beings made from flame, who can adopt various forms (hence the legends about the genie of the bottle that have entranced western, as well as eastern, audiences). There are good and bad *jinn*. Some help human beings, and others meddle harmfully in their affairs. The Qur'ān speaks to *jinn*, as well as to humans (72: 1–8).

Some qur'ānic commentators are aware of the difficulties of reconciling stories about angels and *jinn*; for example, how is it that the *jinn* are sometimes visible to human beings, but often not? Yusuf Ali suggests that the *jinn* might be either spirits, or strangers to Arabia (1975, n. 5728). This is perhaps to miss the point that the qur'ānic accounts of angels and *jinn* locate them and human beings in a more open-ended arena than modern western notions of a natural world from which the supernatural and supranatural are barred. The world is mysterious, filled with things seen and unseen, whose origins may lie beyond the horizon of senses and knowledge. It is not a world that can be mechanistically described by modern science, as though that said everything about it.

Yet, precisely because of the world's inscrutableness and uncertainty, the 'clear sign' of the Qur'ān is needed, not to reduce it to the controllable, but rather to provide within it sure guidance for humans and others. Moreover, although the Qur'ān is chiefly a guidance for human beings, these accounts of angels and *jinn* remind people that God's interest and concern range more widely. Humans need to know this, because of the important role God has given them as his vicegerents, which gives them power over other created things.

Human beings as God's vicegerents

When he created the first man, Adam, God told the angels that he would make him vicegerent on earth (2: 30–34). The Arabic word is *khalīfah*, which means 'successor'. The angels were unimpressed with this news, asking God why he wanted to put there a mischief-maker and shedder of blood, while they praised him. God told them he knew more than they did. It may be that the angels acted out of objective goodness, merely pointing out to God the trouble humans would cause him, each other, and the rest of creation. More likely, the angels were jealous.

Humans are the 'successor' of God in the sense of having more of his knowledge, and thereby power, than the angels and other sentient beings. God taught Adam the name of all things, which gave him power and authority over them. The angels were unable to tell God the name of the man, but he was able to tell God who they were. Whereupon God ordered them to bow down to man, and they did so. Only *'Iblīs*, the devil, disobeyed. *'Iblīs* seems to be described in the Qur'ān as both one of the *jinn* and one of the angels. Like the *jinn*, he is made out of fire, whereas angels are made from light. But he was cast down by God because, alone among the angels, he refused to acknowledge God's new creation, man, made out of clay (2: 34). He tempted Adam and his wife in the garden, which is a spiritual, supra-mundane place of innocency and bliss (2: 19–25). They succumbed to his whisperings, and were expelled from it to the earth, which is now the dwelling place for human beings.

But God then relented, teaching Adam and giving him, and all humans, guidance. Those who follow such guidance have nothing to fear, but those who reject it will go to hell.

Obviously, there are close similarities here with the story of the creation of human beings recounted in the opening book of the Bible. But there are significant differences of emphasis. The qur'ānic account preserves more strongly the sense of God's sovereignty: in the Qur'ān, he teaches Adam the name of things; in Genesis, Adam names them. There is, therefore, a strong sense in Islam of God's complete control over things, so that he delegates 'successorship' to human beings only within seriously prescribed limits. The oft-quoted 'throne-verse' says, of all God's creatures, including human beings: 'they grasp of his [God's] knowledge only what he wills' (2: 255). Moreover, compared with Christian teaching of the Fall, the expulsion from the garden is less cataclysmic. In the New Testament book of Romans, Paul interprets all nature as caught up in the first man's disobedience, groaning in pain and bondage (Rom. 8: 19–22). Islam has no sense of humanity's fall. To be sure, the created order may suffer or benefit from humanity's vicegerency, but the world is not an arena in which a tragic drama of fall, atonement and salvation is played out, involving the whole of creation. Rather, human beings are forgetful of their duty to God, and need guidance to remind them how to fulfil God's will for themselves and their environment.

Why were human beings appointed as God's *khalīfah*? There is a clue to the answer to this question in a statement about David, the biblical figure who appears in the Qur'ān as a prophet. God said to him: 'David. We have appointed you a successor on earth; so judge truthfully between men. Don't follow desires that lead you from God's path' (38: 26). David has to act in an ethical manner.

Humans are ethical beings, able to make moral choices, unlike the majority of God's creation. Some make the wrong choices, and wreak havoc upon others and the environment:

> There is the sort of person whose views on worldly life may beguile you. He calls on God to witness what is in his heart. Yet he is the most militant of enemies. When he leaves you, his aim is to go everywhere spreading discord through the earth, and destroying crops and cattle. God does not love discord. When he is told, 'Fear God', arrogance leads him into sin. Hell awaits him, an evil resting place.
>
> (2: 204–6)

Some communities of people, however, worship God and are his 'successors', in the sense that they seek to know and do his will. According to the Qur'ān, although some Jews have gone astray from his will, among them are others 'who pray regularly, and give the poor-tax, who believe in God and the Last Day' (4: 162). Similarly, although Christians have compromised their belief in God's unity by their worship of Jesus, many are good people. They are 'nearest in love to Muslims . . . Among them are men diligent in learning, who have renounced the world, and they are not arrogant' (5: 85).

What is needed, however, is a community which will more perfectly obey God's moral law. Muslims have aspired to be such a society. In a late qur'ānic passage, which makes mention of Islam as a community of faithful people, God says: 'Let there be from among you a group of people who command the good (*mar'ūf*) and prohibit the evil (*munkar*) (3: 104). The word for good (*mar'ūf*) is mentioned thirty-nine times in the Qur'ān. Muslims are to exercise their 'successorship' to God, by doing good to the rest of creation.

Science

Islam has a long history of interest in the scientific quest. By translating many of the classical Greek and Latin texts into Arabic in the European Middle Ages, Muslim scholars preserved some of the earliest achievements in this field. Many of these texts were then translated from Arabic into European languages, and thus contributed towards the Renaissance and its explosion of knowledge and achievements. From the beginning of Islam to the European Renaissance, a period of 800 years, Muslims were pre-eminent in the fields of medicine and pharmacology, natural history, mathematics and physics. They also explored alchemy, the occult and other activities thought, in their day, to be among the sciences.

Why were Muslims committed to the pursuit of the sciences? The contemporary Iranian scholar, Seyyed Hossein Nasr has written that 'the Qur'ān and the *Ḥadīth* have created an atmosphere for the cultivation of the sciences by emphasising the virtue of all knowledge that is in one way or another a Confirmation of Divine Unity' (Nasr 1976: 5). The Arabic word for knowledge is *'ilm*. The Arabic root from which *'ilm* derives occurs, in all its variant forms, approximately 750 times in the Qur'ān. A tradition records that Muhammad enjoined that knowledge should be sought even as far as China. In Muslim theology, *'ilm* always means *religious* knowledge. This should not be interpreted to mean that Muslims give secondary importance to secular knowledge. Rather, they believe that all knowledge has a religious dimension. Whatever human beings learn has been created by God. In particular, Muslims believe that God has made the wonders which science describes. They do not find a role for God in the areas of life which science cannot explain. Instead, as scientists uncover more and more details about how the universe works (rather than discover, since they are already there!), so the splendour and majesty and inimitability of God, the universal lawgiver, are unveiled.

This point of view contrasts strongly with the philosophy of science widespread in Europe and America since the eighteenth century. Most Muslims regard western science as not so much Christian as secular and profane, unconcerned with God and his will. Such a view of the autonomy of science has, in their judgement, led to a widespread abuse of the natural world among many western scientists, who regard it as a laboratory for their often irresponsible experiments. Muslims believe that science and its practitioners have a more limited scope: they reveal the unity of God as they explore the unity of the created order; and they reverence what they explore as God's handiwork, given purpose and order by him.

In his many works on the subject of Islam and science, Seyyid Hossein Nasr has argued two other important points. First, Muslims have always lived in equilibrium with nature and their environment. Even when they moved from a desert to towns and cities, their sense of the unity and rhythm of creation did not fail them. For example, the architecture and planning of cities took into account natural forces upon which human life depends, such as water, air and light:

> Where there are hot deserts, narrow streets were built to protect the cool air of the night during the daylight hours. Where the temperature became very warm, such as around the central desert (Kavir) of Persia, use was made of wind towers to ventilate homes, of deep basements to serve as places of refuge for the summer and of deep underground cisterns to provide cool water.
>
> (Nasr 1976: 229)

Nasr's other point is that this respect for the equilibrium of the natural world has led Muslims to live at peace in it, despite their conviction that this world is but an antechamber to the next. This is because Muslims respect and obey the law of God, and so will not plunder what has been created by him to be used carefully and reverently. Conversely, modern western science has often been anti-religious, or at least believed God to be irrelevant. Muslims believe that when human beings abandon God they become marauders and not trustees.

Although God creates the laws of nature, he is not bound by them. The Qur'ān leaves a place for miracles: some of the prophets performed miracles, especially Jesus, who made birds out of clay, healed those born blind, cured lepers, and raised the dead – all by God's permission (5: 113). Others, including Muhammad, did not (6: 37; 40: 78). There are traditions that on one occasion the moon was split apart on either side of a mountain near Makkah to impress its pagan inhabitants (Muslim; in Siddiqi 1977, vol. 4, nos 6724–30), but many Muslims regard this as a legend. For them, the Qur'ān is without peer, an incomparable miracle of revelation (10: 37 f.), greater than any miracle of nature. Revelation is itself a great irruption into human life, which offends those who believe in a 'closed universe', sealed against anything that is not explicable by laws derived from within the natural order. Islam believes that humanity needs the guidance scripture brings. Yet God is not unreliable or mischievous. For the most part the universe is dependable and miracles do not happen, not because God does not exist or is an absentee landlord, but because this dependability gives human beings the environment in which they can choose to obey or disregard God's laws. Equally, God's care for human beings means that his laws, even the laws of nature, are not immutable ends in themselves, but serve his desire to enable people to discern his presence and obey his will.

Animals

According to the Qur'ān, 'there is not an animal on earth, nor a bird that flies on its wings – but they are communities like you . . . and they shall all be gathered to their Lord in the end' (6: 38). This means that they fulfil the plan which God has allotted to them in his purpose. They are not to be treated as valueless by human beings. It has not usually been taken by commentators of the Qur'ān or jurists to mean that animals share in the bliss (or torment) of life after death. Human beings are distinguished from animals by their capacity to make moral judgements. Only they, of all species of life, can choose to obey or disobey God, and so earn paradise or hell.

Islam is not a sentimental religion. By God's permission, human beings have power over the animals, as over all creation, and they can be used for various purposes:

> He has created cattle for you. You get from them warmth and many benefits, and food. And you derive pride from driving them home at night, and leading them to pasture in the morning. They carry your burdens to lands you could not reach except with great trouble. Your Lord is full of kindness and mercy. There are horses, mules and donkeys, for you to ride or for show.
>
> (16: 5–8)

The emphasis in this passage is on the practical use of animals, but the last part indicates that some animals may be kept to give pleasure. Islam forbids the keeping of some animals for domestic purposes. Most Muslims do not have dogs as pets. According to traditions of the Prophet, he ordered the killing of dogs in Madinah, and warned that anyone who kept dogs other than to protect property or hunt would be debited good works from their balance sheet by God. This would count against them on the Day of Judgement (Muslim, in Siddiqi 1977, vol. 3, nos 3809–29). Muhammad did not like dogs. He is reported to have said: 'Were dogs not a species of creature I should command that they all be killed; but kill every pure black one' (Robson 1970, vol. 2: 876). However, he did not mean that dogs could be mistreated. A prostitute who saw a thirsty dog hanging around a well one day, gave it water to drink. For this act of kindness, the Prophet pardoned all her sins. Conversely, a woman who had tied up a cat and not provided it with food or drink until it died was thrown into hell (Muslim, in Siddiqi 1977, vol. 4, nos 5570–76).

Other traditions of the Prophet forbid treating animals cruelly. They are not to be caged, or beaten unnecessarily, or branded on the face, or allowed to fight each other for human entertainment. They must not be mutilated while they are alive, which forbids vivisection. Muslims are opposed to battery farming, the slaughter of calves for veal, and all other forms of animal-husbandry which are cruel to creatures or which needlessly kill them. These interdicts arise out of the Islamic emphasis that human beings have a moral obligation towards animals.

Animals can be hunted only for food, not for sport. The Prophet once said:

> 'If anyone kills a sparrow or anything greater wrongfully God will question him about killing it.' On being asked what was the right way he

replied, 'To cut its throat and eat it, but not cut off its head and throw it away'.

(Robson 1970, vol. 2: 874)

A very important function of animals is to provide human beings with food. Few Muslims are vegetarians. But certain animals are forbidden to Muslims, and all creatures used for food need to be killed in a prescribed manner.

Islamic law declares certain things permissible (*ḥalāl*) for human beings, and other things harmful (*ḥarām*). This division covers all aspects of life, including what Muslims can eat. Muslims regard all things as *ḥalāl* unless God has commanded otherwise. There are four forbidden categories of food, which are derived from the Qur'ān (5: 4):

1. meat of dead animals
2. blood
3. pigs' flesh
4. meat over which another name than God's has been invoked.

The meat of dead animals is taken to mean a beast or fowl which dies of natural causes, without being slaughtered or hunted by humans. The qur'ānic verse offers five classifications of dead animals:

1. the strangled
2. those beaten to death
3. those fallen from a height
4. those gored by other animals
5. those partly eaten by wild animals.

Scholars have elaborated a number of reasons for this prohibition. The animal might have died of some disease. Muslims should intend to kill an animal for food, offering it to God, and not thoughtlessly make use of a deceased creature. By this ban, God makes food available to other animals and birds.

Islamic law has exempted fish, whales and other sea-creatures from the category of dead animals. The Qur'ān says: 'The game of the sea is permitted to you and so is its food' (5: 99). Traditions relate that the Prophet allowed dead food that comes from the sea to be eaten. One story tells of a group of Muslims sent by Muhammad to ambush his enemies. They became very hungry, until the sea threw out a huge, dead whale. They ate its meat, rubbed their bodies with its fat, and, when one of its ribs was fixed over the ground, a rider passed beneath it (Bukhari, in Khan 1984, vol. 7: 293 f.). Many jurists have amplified this permission so that all marine creatures, those which live in the sea and cannot survive outside it, are *ḥalāl*. It does not matter whether they are taken from the water dead or living, whole or in bits, whether they are caught by a Muslim or someone else.

The interdict on blood is interpreted to mean flowing blood, which was felt by jurists to be repugnant and injurious to health. The law does not forbid eating blood that remains in the animal after the flow has ceased.

Pork is outlawed on a number of grounds. It is dangerous to eat in hot climates, where it quickly goes off. It is regarded as an unclean animal, eating filth and offal, and so its meat is repugnant to decent people. Some scholars have claimed that it incites those who eat it to shameful and lustful thoughts.

Finally, God's name must be invoked when the animal is slaughtered. The man who slits its throat says: *bi-smillāhi, allāhu akbar*, 'in the name of God, God is most great'. It is not acceptable to invoke the name of an idol, as Arab polytheists at the time of Muhammad did. Nor is it all right to say nothing. Killing an animal for food is a devotional act. God gave humans control over all the earth, subjecting animals to them, and allowing them to take an animal's life for food. Pronouncing God's name while killing the creature is a reminder of God's permission and ultimate control over all things.

Other than these four categories, all food can be eaten and enjoyed (2: 172; 6: 119). Indeed, the emphasis in Islam is upon what can be eaten and enjoyed, rather than on what is forbidden. Only a few things are forbidden. There is no virtue in exceedingly strict food laws. According to a widespread interpretation of qur'ānic teaching, the more restrictive Jewish food laws are the consequence of disobedience: 'Because of the wrongdoing of the Jews, We made unlawful certain good and wholesome things [usually taken to mean foods], which had previously been allowed them' (4: 160).

Under certain circumstances, even meat in the four forbidden categories can be eaten – 6: 119 mentions the banned groups, and then adds: 'But if one is compelled by necessity, without wanting to disobey or transgressing then he is sinless. God is forgiving, merciful'. A consensus of the jurists is that necessity means when no other food is available. Some hold that at least a day and a night should pass without food, then one may eat from these categories.

One other forbidden category is mentioned in many books of Sunni law, that of four-footed animals who seize their prey with their teeth and birds which grip it with their talons. In effect, this forbids Muslims from eating any flesh-eating creature, for example, hyenas, foxes, kites, crows.

Land animals that are *ḥalāl* are of two types: domesticated and wild. Islamic law requires domesticated animals to be slaughtered in a prescribed manner. They are to be killed by a sharp object that can sever blood vessels. The best way is to cut the windpipe, gullet and two jugular veins. In effect, this means a clean cut across the throat, from side to side. The name of God must be mentioned at the time of slaughter, and no other name. Muslims believe that this method is the quickest and least painful for the animal. In villages in many parts of the Muslim world, animals are killed by each head of the family. In Britain, a special licence is needed to kill animals, so there are *ḥalāl* slaughterhouses, as there are in many towns and cities in Muslim-majority countries. Some of these places differ from non-Muslim abbatoirs, because Muslim law forbids slaying an animal in the presence of other creatures, so as not to distress them unduly.

Wild animals are killed by hunting, and they become *ḥalāl* in a rather different way than domesticated animals. As the circumstances of the hunt permit, some variation on cutting the animal's throat is allowed. For example, if the caught animal is wounded but still alive, then its throat must be slit. If it is dead, then it may still be eaten. The Prophet said: 'When you shoot your arrow, and the animal goes out of your sight, eat it when you come upon it, provided it has not a stench' (Robson 1970, vol. 2: 871). The hunter must be a Muslim or, some scholars concede, another kind of monotheist.

Although some jurists argue that it is permitted to eat meat offered by Christians and Jews, unless the name of Jesus or some other person was mentioned at the time of slaughter, few Muslims will eat meat offered by Christians, who are regarded as imperfect monotheists. However, some jurists even allow food killed for

Christian festivals, regarding it as *makrūh* – disapproved though not actually forbidden. When Jews, Christians and other monotheists kill in their way, perhaps by electric shock, such meat is considered *ḥalāl* for Muslims by some jurists. The Prophet was generous in his interpretation of what was allowed:

> A'isha [a wife of the Prophet] told that some people said, 'Messenger of God, there are people here, recent converts from polytheism, who bring us meat and we do not know whether or not they mention God's name over it.' He replied, 'Mention God's name yourselves and eat'.
>
> (Robson 1970, vol. 2: 871)

The rule appears to be: what we do not see should not be probed into. Even so, many Muslims will only eat meat they are more certain about. This greatly affects the Muslims' ability to eat with their non-Muslim neighbours. Although many Muslims will not, in conscience, eat their neighbours' meat, they offer hospitality to them. Also, it is possible to eat vegetarian food together and, in Britain, there are an increasing number of *ḥalāl* butchers, who are happy to sell to non-Muslims.

Nowadays, the ritual killing of animals is condemned by many non-Muslim individuals and groups. The bottom line for Muslims is that it is commanded by God, and this order counts for more than the opinions of others. Muslims are not mawkish about such matters. Islam began on the fringes of the desert, where staying alive was the pre-eminent concern of many people, and meat was regarded by them as a necessity, not a luxury. Most Muslims today live in relatively poor countries, where survival counts for more than middle-class values, which can seem excessively indulgent. Islam gives human beings power over, and responsibility for, animals, which should be treated with kindness and consideration, but which, by God's permission, provide food, clothing and transport.

Green Islam

Islam's characteristic lack of sentimentality extends to its views about ecology. Many Muslims regard the western world's conversion to green issues with scepticism and contempt. It was the West that, through modern technology and political and economic control of wide areas of this planet, despoiled nature, and probably contributed towards global warming. Muslims in poor countries have not had the means to wreak such havoc on the environment.

Nevertheless, Muslims are expected to treat their environment with respect. They take seriously the qur'ānic observation that: 'Corruption has appeared on land and sea because of what human hands have done' (30: 41). But, as the community charged with obeying God more perfectly than others, Muslims must follow a higher ideal.

Upon what religious grounds do Muslims base their concern for the environment? The Qur'ān describes (55: 7) how 'God has lifted the heavens up high, and has set up the balance' (*mīzān*). The word *mīzān* is often used figuratively in the Qur'ān: as the scales on which the deeds of people will be weighed on the Day of Judgement (21: 47), or as the revelation contained in scripture (42: 16) which enables people to weigh all moral issues. In 55: 8 and 9, *mīzān* may refer to the need for people to act justly, with balance, towards one another. Some modern Muslims, however, see 55: 7 as indicating that the world is delicately balanced by God. Only as such a balance is preserved by people will they properly obey the will of God. To destroy the balance of nature by an abuse of science and technology is, therefore, ungodly. Such a reading of the verse is highly relevant in our modern world. However, it is a controversial interpretation of that verse. There are better grounds on which to establish Islam's green credentials.

These grounds are Islam's laws about the use of natural resources, of which the most important are land and water. Islam divides land into three main categories: developed, undeveloped and 'protective zones'. These establish rules of ownership, and thereby, of responsibilities that devolve from ownership. Undeveloped land offers an interesting example of Islam's insistence on the creative and fruitful use of natural resources. All major manuals of Muslim law contain sections on 'bringing dead lands to life'. This can be achieved in one of these ways:

- putting a hedge or wall around the land
- irrigating it (if it is too dry) or draining it (if too wet)
- digging a well or making a spring
- clearing the area of trees, stones and the like
- tilling or ploughing the land

- planting on it
- erecting a building there.

Such treatment of the land leads to rights of ownership; responsibility and proprietorship are linked in Muslim law.

Similarly, this law applies to water. Water is, in its natural state, common property. But rights of ownership fall upon those who have, for example, dug a well on their private land.

Mineral deposits are of two kinds: open (*ẓāhir*) and concealed (*bāṭin*). The former include salt and all minerals that are easily worked, and open to all who come for them. The latter include metals and oil, for which work is needed to remove the product. There are differences of opinion among jurists about who owns these, and whether such ownership is total, or merely extends to the right of usufruct during one's life.

However, the basic point is that minerals, land and water – the earth's resources – are for the use of everyone, but are entrusted to those who care for them. They are God's precious gifts, to be esteemed and tended carefully and not to be squandered.[7]

Some Muslim individuals and governments do not live up to Islam's high ideals. In particular, the use of oil by some Muslims for personal wealth and aggrandisement, or for their country's economic and political dominance, is offensive to many of their co-religionists. There is also a lively debate about the possession and possible use of nuclear weapons. Some Muslims think that, because non-Muslim governments have them, Muslim countries are permitted to, so as to be able adequately to defend themselves and Islam. But many Muslims think that the creation of nuclear weapons involves an irresponsible and ungodly use of the earth's natural resources, which could be used for more humane and godly purposes.

The planet earth: a temporary home

Our lived and experienced environment, however, is not eternal, to be cherished and safeguarded because it is all we have. One day, God, who created it, will destroy it: 'all that is on earth will pass away, but the face of your Lord will abide' (55: 26 f.).

God has ordained *yawm al-Qiyāmah*, the Day of Judgement. The cataclysmic events of this day are graphically described in the Qur'ān. Each human being will end up either in heaven or in hell.

This process involves the end of this world and solar system, as *sūrahs* 81 and 82 of the Qur'ān vividly portray: the former *sūrah* is called *Takwīr*, or 'the Folding Up', and the latter *Infiṭār*, or 'the cleaving asunder'. But even though this chaos is vividly depicted, the destruction of the created order is not the primary focus. Rather, the destiny of human beings takes centre stage:

> When the sky is torn apart, and the heavenly bodies scattered; when the seas burst their bonds, and the graves are overturned: each soul shall know what it has put forward [in goodness] and what it has kept back.
>
> (82: 1–5)

This earthly and planetary environment has no eternal future; it is the nurturing home for human beings, who do have a future, in heaven or hell. When the solar system has fulfilled that purpose, it will cease to exist. Whether the language, both of the Qur'ān and the *Ḥadīth* literature, is literal or metaphorical, it is the idiom of destruction:

> 'The world is like a garment torn from end to end and hanging by a thread at the end of it; and that thread will soon be cut off . . . The sun and moon will be folded up on the day of resurrection'.
>
> (Robson 1970, vol. 2: 1162, 1166)

NOTES

1. Muslims always refer to the Prophet Muhammad with great respect. When they write in English, they usually put PBUH ('peace be upon him') in brackets after his name.
2. AH means 'Anno Hegirae' (the year of the *hijrah*), the 'emigration' by Muhammad and his followers from Makkah to Madinah in 622 CE. Muslims date their calendar from this event. They follow a lunar year, which is shorter than the solar year of the Common (or Christian) Era. We have used the Common Era dating in the text.
3. More detailed information about the process behind the formation of Islamic law is given in the chapter on Islam in the book of this series entitled *Sacred Writings*.
4. It is difficult to choose a good English translation of the Qu'rān for various reasons that are described in the chapter on Islam in the book

of this series entitled *Sacred Writings*. We have sometimes offered our own translation, or else used that by A. Yusuf Ali, first published in 1934 and now available from many publishers. It has the advantage of 6310 mostly helpful footnotes, though the text, like so many translations, betrays the influence of the King James 'authorised' version of the Bible in the use of an old-fashioned English that was felt to be reverential.

5. Maududi, A.A. (1940) *Towards Understanding Islam*, Lahore, Idara Tarjuman-ul-Quran, 2 f.
6. Miracles are dealt with in the section on Science. A discussion of the importance of prophets and the Qu'rān is found in the chapter on Islam in the book in this series, *Sacred Writings*.
7. For information about the use of natural resources, we are indebted to Yassin Dutton's article in Khalid and O'Brien (eds) 1992: 51–67.

FURTHER READING

Khalid, F. with O'Brien, J. (eds) (1992) *Islam and Ecology*, London, Cassell.

Khan, M.M. (ed.) (1984) *Sahah Al-Bukhari*, vols 1–9, Delhi, Kitab Bhavan.

Nasr, S.H. (1976) *Islamic Science: an illustrated study*, London, Thames and Hudson.

Robson, J.R. (1970 edn) *Mishkat al-Masibih*, vols 1–2, Lahore, Muhammad Ashraf.

Siddiqi, A.H. (ed.) (1977) *Sahih Muslim*, vols 1–4, Delhi, Kitab Bhavan.

Yusuf Ali, A. (1975 edn) *The Holy Qu'rān: Text, Translation and Commentary*, Leicester, Islamic Foundation.

The works of Khan, Robson and Siddiqi are all English translations, available from specialised South Asian and Muslim bookshops in the United Kingdom.

5. Judaism

Norman Solomon

It is widely recognised today that people are destroying the environment on which living things depend for their existence. It is not at first sight clear what the problems facing the earth's environment have to do with religious beliefs. After all, the only belief necessary to motivate a constructive response to them is a belief in the desirability of human survival, wedded to the perception that human survival depends on the whole interlinking system of nature. Moreover, the discovery of which procedures would effectively solve the problems of conservation is a technical, not a religious one. If scientists are able to offer alternative procedures of the same or different efficiency, the religious may feel that the ethical or spiritual values they espouse should determine the choice. However, few choices depend on value judgements alone, and no judgement is helpful which is not based on the best available scientific information.

These considerations will be borne in mind as we examine the relevance of traditional Jewish sources to our theme. In the following pages we offer a structured guide to the main traditional Jewish sources which relate to the great environmental problems of our time (concluding with a model Jewish statement on nature). Judaism did not 'stop' with the Bible or the Talmud; it is a living religion, constantly developing in response to changing social realities and intellectual perceptions. At the present time, it is passing through one of its most creative phases; however, within the limited scope of this chapter only a few references can be made to the contemporary literature.

Traditional Jewish thought is expressed in several complementary genres. The most distinctive is *halakhah*, or law, but history, myth, poetry, philosophy and other forms of expression are also significant. Our focus here is not on the contributions made by individual Jews, for instance scientists and economists, to the modern ecological movement – this would make an interesting study in itself – but on the religious sources, which demonstrate the continuity between traditional Jewish thought and a range of contemporary approaches.

Attitudes to creation

GOODNESS OF THE PHYSICAL WORLD

'God saw that it was good' is the refrain of the first creation story of Genesis (1: 1–2: 4), which includes the physical creation of humankind, male and female. The created world is thus testimony to God's goodness and greatness (see Pss. 8, 104, 148; Job 36: 22–41: 34).

For the ordinary Jew, this goodness of creation is encapsulated in the blessing to be recited on seeing the first blossoms in spring:

> You are blessed, Lord our God and ruler of the universe, who have omitted nothing from your world, but created within it good creatures and good and beautiful trees in which people may take delight.
>
> (Prayer Book)

The second 'creation' story (Gen. 2: 5–3: 24) accounts for the psychological make-up of humankind. There is no devil, only a 'wily serpent', and the excuse of being misled by the serpent does not exempt Adam and Eve from personal responsibility for what they have done. Bad gets into the world through the free exercise of choice by people, not in the process of creation, certainly not through fallen angels, devils, or any other external projection of human guilt; such creatures are notably absent from the catalogue of creation in Genesis 1.

Post-biblical Judaism did not adopt the concept of 'the devil'. In the Middle Ages, however, the dualism of body and spirit prevailed, and with it a tendency to denigrate 'this world' and 'material things'. The Palestinian kabbalist, Isaac Luria (1534–72), taught that God initiated the process of creation by 'withdrawing' himself from the infinite space he occupied; this theory stresses the 'inferiority' and distance from God of material creation, but compensates by drawing attention to the divine element concealed in all things. The modern Jewish theologian who wishes to emphasise the inherent goodness of God's creation has not only the resources of the Hebrew scriptures on which to draw, but a continuous tradition based on them.

The Bible encompasses three realms: of God, of humankind and of nature. It does not confuse them. Its 'creation spirituality' articulates 'original blessing' rather than 'original sin' – 'God saw all that he had made, and it was very good' (Gen. 1: 31) – and this includes all creatures, culminating with humans. As Aaron Lichtenstein remarked at a conference on Judaism and Ecology at Bar Ilan University (Tel Aviv), 'Our approach is decidedly anthropocentric, and that is nothing to be ashamed of.'[1]

Below, the section on the hierarchy in creation discusses the hierarchy within nature itself.

BIODIVERSITY

I recall sitting in the synagogue as a child and listening to the reading of Genesis. I was puzzled by the Hebrew word *leminehu*, 'according to its kind', which followed the names of most of the created items and was apparently superfluous. Obviously, if God created fruit with seeds, the seeds were 'according to its kind'!

As time went on I became more puzzled. Scripture seemed obsessive about 'kinds' (species). There were careful lists and definitions of which species of creature might or might not be eaten (Lev. 11 and Deut. 14). Wool and linen were not to be mixed in a garment (Lev. 19: 19; Deut. 22: 11), ox and ass were not to plough together (Deut. 22: 10), fields (Lev. 19: 19) and vineyards (Deut. 22: 9) were not to be sown with mixed seeds, or animals cross-bred (Lev. 19: 19) and, following the rabbinic interpretation of a thrice-repeated biblical phrase (Exod. 23: 19, 34: 26; Deut. 14: 21), meat and milk were not to be cooked or eaten together.

The story of Noah's Ark manifests anxiety that all species should be conserved, irrespective of their usefulness to humankind – Noah is instructed to take into his ark viable (according to the thought of the time) populations of both 'clean' and 'unclean' animals. That is why the 'Inter-stellar Ark' is the model, among those concerned with such things, for gigantic spaceships to carry total, balanced communities of living things through the galaxy for survival or colonisation.

The biblical preoccupation with species and with keeping them distinct can now be read as a way of declaring the 'rightness' of God's pattern for creation and of calling on humankind not only not to interfere with it, but to cherish biodiversity by conserving species.

Scripture does not, of course, take account of the evolution of species, with its postulates of (a) the alteration of species over time and (b) the extinction (long before the evolution of humans) of most species which have so far appeared on earth.[2] Yet at the very least these Hebrew texts assign unique value to each species as it now is, within the context of the present order of creation; this is sufficient to give a religious dimension, within Judaism, to the call to conserve species.

Pereq Shirah

Pereq Shirah (the 'Chapter of Song') affords a remarkable demonstration of the traditional Jewish attitude to nature and its species. No-one knows who composed this 'song', though it may have originated among the *hekhalot* mystics of the fourth or fifth centuries.

More significant than its origin is its actual use in private devotion. It has been associated with the 'Songs of Unity' composed by the German pietists of the twelfth century, who undoubtedly stimulated its popularity. At some stage, copyists prefaced to it exhortatory sayings which were erroneously attributed to talmudic rabbis, for instance: 'Rabbi Eliezer the Great declared that whoever says *pereq shirah* in this world will acquire the right to say it in the world to come'.

As the work is printed today it is divided into five or six sections:

1. the physical creation (this includes heaven and hell, Leviathan and other sea creatures)
2. plants and trees
3. creeping things
4. birds
5. land animals (in some versions this section is subdivided).

Each section consists of from ten to twenty-five biblical verses, each interpreted as the song or saying of some part of creation or of some individual creature. The cock, in the fourth section, is given 'seven voices', and its function in the poem is to link the earthly song, in which all nature praises God, with the heavenly song.

We shall see, in the section: Hierarchy in creation, how the philosopher Albo (1380–1435) drew on *Pereq Shirah* to express the relationship between the human and the animal; yet *pereq shirah* itself draws all creation – even the inanimate, even heaven and hell themselves – into the relationship, expressing a fullness which derives only from the rich diversity of things, and which readily translates into the modern concept of biodiversity.

STEWARDSHIP OR DOMINATION?

There has been discussion among Christian theologians as to whether the opening chapters of Genesis call on humans to act as stewards – guardians of creation – or to dominate and exploit the created world. There is little debate on this point among Jewish theologians,[3] to whom it has always been obvious that when Genesis states that Adam was placed in the garden 'to till it and to care for it' (2: 15) it means just what it says. As Rav Kook (1865–1935)[4] put it:

> No rational person can doubt that the Torah, when it commands people to 'rule over the fishes of the sea and the birds of the sky and all living things that move on the earth' does not have in mind a cruel ruler who exploits his people and servants for his own will and desires – God forbid that such a detestable law of slavery [be attributed to God] who 'is good to all and his tender care rests upon all his creatures' (Ps. 145: 9) and 'the world is built on tender mercy' (Ps. 89: 3).[5,6]

In the twelfth century the great Jewish Bible scholar, Abraham ibn Ezra, commented as follows on the words of Psalm 115: 16, 'The heavens are the heavens of the Lord, and he gave the earth to people':

> The ignorant have compared man's rule over the earth with God's rule over the heavens. This is not right, for God rules over everything. The

> meaning of 'he gave it to people' is that man is God's steward (*paqid* – officer or official with special responsibility for a specific task) over the earth, and must do everything according to God's word.

So perverse is it to understand 'and rule over it' (Gen. 1: 28) – let alone Psalm 8 – as meaning 'exploit and destroy' that many Christians take such interpretations as a deliberate attempt to besmirch Christianity, and not a few Jews have read the discussions as an attempt to 'blame the Jews' for yet another disaster in Christendom. The context of Genesis 1: 28 is indeed that of humans being made in the image of God, the beneficent creator of good things; its meaning is, therefore, very precise – that humans, being in the image of God, are summoned to share in his creative work, and to do all in their power to sustain creation.

HIERARCHY IN CREATION

'God created humans[7] in His image . . . male and female he created them' (Gen. 1: 27). In some sense, humankind is superior to animals, animals to plants, plants to the inanimate. There is a hierarchy in created things.

The hierarchical model has two practical consequences. First, as we have seen, is that of responsibility of the higher for the lower, traditionally expressed as 'rule', latterly as 'stewardship'. The second is that, in a competitive situation, the higher has priority over the lower. Humans have priority over dogs so that, for instance, it is wrong for a man to risk his life to save that of a dog, though right, in many circumstances, for him to risk his life to save that of another human. Contemporary dilemmas arising from this are described below in the section which discusses ethical problems relating to conservation.

The Spanish Jewish philosopher, Joseph Albo (1380–1435), placed humans at the top of the earthly hierarchy, and discerned in this the possibility for humans to receive God's revelation (*Sefer Ha-Iqqarim*, Book III, Ch. 1). This is just a mediaeval way of saying what we have already remarked. God's revelation, as understood by Albo and Jewish tradition, is the Torah, from which we learn our responsibilities to each other and to the rest of creation.

According to Albo, just as clothes are an integral part of the animal, but external to people, who have to make clothes for themselves, so are specific ethical impulses integral to the behaviour of particular animals, and we should learn from their behaviour. 'Who teaches us from the beasts of the earth, and imparts wisdom to us through the birds of the sky?' (Job 35: 11) – as the Talmud puts it: 'R. Yohanan said, If these things were not commanded in the Torah, we could learn modesty from the cat, the ant would preach against robbery, and the dove against incest' (B. *Eruvin* 100b). The superiority of humans lies in their unique combination of freedom to choose and the intelligence to judge, without which the divine revelation would have no application. Being in this sense 'higher' than other creatures, humans must be humble towards all. Albo, in citing these passages and commending the reading of *Pereq Shirah* (see above), articulates the attitude of humble stewardship towards creation which characterises rabbinic Judaism.

Rav Kook, drawing on a range of classical Jewish sources, from Psalm 148 to Lurianic mysticism, beautifully acknowledges the divine significance of all things (the immanence of God):

> I recall that with God's grace in the year 5665 [1904/5] I visited Jaffa in the Holy Land, and went to pay my respects to its Chief Rabbi [Rav Kook]. He received me warmly . . . and after the afternoon prayer I accompanied him as he went out into the fields, as was his wont, to concentrate his thoughts. As we were walking I plucked some flower or plant; he trembled, and quietly told me that he always took great care not to pluck, unless it were for some benefit, anything that could grow, for there was no plant below that did not have its guardian[8] above. Everything that grew said something, every stone whispered some secret, all creation sang.
>
> (Aryeh Levine (1961) *Lahai Roi*, Jerusalem, 5721: 15, 16)

CONCERN FOR ANIMALS

Kindness to animals is a motivating factor for general concern with the environment, rather than itself an element in conservation.

Kindness to animals features prominently in the Jewish tradition. The Ten Commandments include domestic animals in the Sabbath rest:

> Remember to keep the sabbath day holy . . . you shall not do any work, you, your son or your daughter . . . your cattle.
>
> (Exod. 20: 10 NEB)

Early in the third century the rabbis formulated the 'seven Laws of the Children of Noah', which was an attempt to define the religious obligations of humankind in general, for all people are descended from Noah. The laws, unknown in this form in sources earlier than the third century, are: Do not blaspheme, do not worship idols, do not murder, do not commit adultery, do not steal, do establish courts of justice, do not eat 'a limb torn from a living animal'. The last of these covers cruelty to animals, evidently understood as a major human responsibility.[9]

Pious tales and folklore exemplify this attitude.

> A calf was about to be slaughtered. It ran to Rabbi (Judah the Patriarch, about the year 200), nestled its head in his robe and whimpered. He said to it, 'Go! This is what you were created for!' As he did not show it mercy, heaven decreed suffering upon him. One day Rabbi's housekeeper was sweeping. She came across some young weasels and threw them and swept them out; he said, 'Let them alone! Is it not written, "His mercies extend to all his creatures" (Psalm 148: 9)?' Heaven decreed, 'Since he is merciful, let us show him mercy'.
>
> (B. *Bava Metzia* 85a, slightly adapted)

The folk tale of the Rabbi and the Frog, a long and strange tale of how the rabbi was rewarded for his kindness to the amphibian, illustrates popular Jewish thought in the Middle Ages on this matter (Moses E. Gaster (ed.) (1934) *Maaseh Book* Vol. I, Jewish Publication Society of America).

Causing pain or distress to animals

In rabbinic law this concern condenses into the concept of *tsaar baalei hayyim* ('distress to living creatures').[10] An illuminating instance of halakhic concern for animal welfare is the rule attributed to the third century Babylonian Rav that one should feed one's cattle before breaking bread oneself (B. *Berakhot* 40a); even the Sabbath laws are relaxed somewhat to enable rescue of injured animals or milking of cows to ease their distress. Recently, concern has been expressed about intensive animal husbandry, including battery chicken production (Shochet 1984). Likewise, many rabbinic Responsa have been published on the restraints to be placed on experimentation on animals; clearly, experimentation is not allowed for frivolous purposes, but it is necessary to define both the human benefits which might justify animal experimentation and the safeguards necessary to avoid unnecessary suffering to animals. (See Bleich, 1989, for a review of the halakhic literature on animal experimentation.)

Meat eating

The Torah does not enjoin vegetarianism, though Adam and Eve were vegetarian (Gen. 1: 29). Restrictions on meat eating perhaps indicate that it is a concession to human weakness; among the mediaeval Jewish philosophers of the Iberian peninsula, Joseph Albo (1380–1435) wrote that the first people were forbidden to eat meat because of the cruelty involved in killing animals (*Sefer Ha-Iqqarim* 3: 15). Isaac Abravanel (1437–1508) endorsed this in his commentary on Isaiah, Ch. 11 and also taught in his commentary on Genesis, Ch. 2, that when the Messiah comes we would return to the ideal, vegetarian state. Today the popular trend to vegetarianism has won many Jewish adherents though little official backing from religious leaders.[11]

Although the Torah does not insist on vegetarianism, it places considerable restraints on the eating of meat; only the meat of certain animals may be eaten, certain parts may not be eaten at all, the blood must be drained, and there are regulations as to how the animals should be slaughtered. *Shehitah*, the method of slaughter, is by a single sharp cut across the trachaea and oesophagus; this may be performed only by a qualified religious expert, and nowadays there are special pens and procedures to ensure that the animal suffers the minimum of psychological distress as well as the minimum pain. Since in any case the animal very swiftly loses consciousness, generally before the onset of pain from the sharp cut, this is a very humane process.

From time to time voices are heard suggesting that *shehitah* is cruel to animals, but the criticisms often concern inessential aspects of *shehitah*, such as the form of casting-pen used, rather than *shehitah* itself. Nevertheless, there is at least a theoretical problem for Jews of what to do should it be demonstrated that the *shehitah* process is to some extent cruel; there would be a contradiction between two equally clear demands of Torah, that meat not be eaten unless *shehitah* has been correctly performed, and that one should not practise cruelty to animals. Since the only cruelty which could conceivably be demonstrated would be minor, it is probable that the decision reached would be that *shehitah* be continued, and the procedures improved as far as possible; otherwise, orthodox Jews would be forced to be vegetarians. Judaism does not recognise cruelty to animals as an absolute value (see section: Animal versus human life); any *prima facie* instance must be evaluated as to its seriousness and then balanced against alternatives.

Judah Tiktin[12] cites the kabbalist Isaac Luria (1534–72) as saying 'Happy are they who are able to abstain from eating meat and drinking wine throughout the week'. This has been cited as support for vegetarianism, but is irrelevant. The context is that of abstaining from meat and wine on Mondays and Thursdays (the traditional penitential days), a custom akin to the once widespread Roman Catholic practice of not eating meat on Fridays. The goal is self-denial, or asceticism, not vegetarianism, as may be inferred from the fact that the very same authorities endorse the eating of meat and the drinking of wine in moderation as the appropriate way to celebrate the Sabbath and festivals. There have, indeed, been some holy men whose asceticism has led them to abstain entirely from eating meat and drinking wine – Rabbi Joseph Kahaneman (1888–1969) for instance – but this provides no basis in principle for vegetarianism.

Hunting

On 23 February 1716 Duke Christian of Sachsen Weissenfels celebrated his fifty-third birthday by a great hunting party. History would have passed by the Duke as well as the occasion had not J.S. Bach honoured them with his 'Hunting Cantata'. The text by Salomo Franck, secretary of the upper consistory at Weimar, is a grand celebration of nature and its priest, Duke Christian, with no sense that hunting sounds a discordant note, and the cantata includes one of Bach's most expressive arias, *Schafe können sicher weiden* ('Sheep may safely graze').

Hunting, it has been argued, enhances appreciation of nature. Moreover, the hunter does not oppose conservation; he destroys only individual prey but has an interest in preserving the species.

Conditions of Jewish life in the past millennium or so have rarely afforded Jewish princes the opportunity to celebrate their birthdays by hunting parties. But it has happened from time to time and has led rabbis, the best known being Ezekiel Landau (1713–93), rabbi of Prague, to voice their censure.

Professor Nahum Rakover,[13] Deputy Attorney General of Israel, sums up the halakhic objections to 'sport' hunting under eight heads:

1. It is destructive/wasteful (see section: Cutting down fruit trees).
2. It causes distress to animals (see section: Causing pain or distress to animals).
3. It actively produces non-kosher carcasses (since the prey, even if a kosher animal, will not have been slaughtered lawfully).
4. It leads to trading non-kosher commodities.
5. The hunter exposes himself to danger unnecessarily.
6. It wastes time (which should be devoted to study and good deeds).
7. The hunt is a 'seat of the scornful' (Ps. 1: 1).[14]
8. 'Thou shalt not conform to their institutions' (Lev. 18: 3) (i.e. hunting is contrary to the Jewish ethos).

From this we see that although Jewish religious tradition despises hunting for sport, this is on ethical and ritual grounds rather than in the interest of conservation.

The land and the people – a paradigm

Judaism, while attentive to the universal significance of its essential teachings, has developed within a specific context of a people bound by covenant with God. In the Bible itself, the most obvious feature of this is the stress on the chosen people and the chosen land.

This has meant that Judaism, both in biblical times and subsequently, has emphasised the interrelationship of people and land, the idea that the prosperity of the land depends on the people's obedience to God's covenant. For instance:

> If you pay heed to the commandments which I give you this day, and love the Lord your God and serve him with all your heart and soul, then I will send rain for your land in season . . . and you will gather your

> corn and new wine and oil, and I will provide pasture . . . you shall eat your fill. Take good care not to be led astray in your hearts nor to turn aside and serve other gods . . . or the Lord will become angry with you; he will shut up the skies and there will be no rain, your ground will not yield its harvest, and you will soon vanish from the rich land which the Lord is giving you.
>
> (Deut. 11: 13–17)

Two steps are necessary to apply this link between morality and prosperity to the contemporary situation:

1. The chosen land and people must be understood as the prototype of:
   (a) all actual individual geographical nations (including, of course, Israel) in their relationships with land, and
   (b) humanity as a whole in its relationship with the planet as a whole.
2. There must be satisfactory clarification of the meaning of 'obedience to God' as the human side of the covenant to ensure that 'the land will be blessed'. The Bible certainly has in mind justice and moral rectitude, but in spelling out 'the commandments of God' it includes specific prescriptions which directly regulate care of the land and celebration of its produce; some of these are discussed below.

To sum up – the Bible stresses the intimate relationship between people and land. The prosperity of land depends on:

1. the social justice and moral integrity of the people on it, and
2. a caring, even loving, attitude to land, with effective regulation of its use.

Conservation demands the extrapolation of these principles from ancient or idealised Israel to the contemporary global situation; this calls for education in social values together with scientific investigation of the effects of our activities on nature.

SABBATICAL YEAR AND JUBILEE

> When you enter the land which I give you, the land shall keep sabbaths to the Lord. For six years you may sow your fields and for six years prune your vineyards but in the seventh year the land shall keep a sabbath of sacred rest, a sabbath to the Lord. You shall not sow your field nor prune your vineyard.
>
> Lev. 25: 2–4)

The analogy between the sabbath (literally, 'rest day') of the land and that of people communicates the idea that land must 'rest' to be refreshed and regain its productive vigour. In contemporary terms, land resources must be conserved through the avoidance of over-use.

The Bible pointedly links this to social justice. Just as land must not be exploited, so slaves must go free after six years of bondage or in the Jubilee (fiftieth) year, and the sabbatical year (in Hebrew *shemittah* – 'release') cancels private debts, thus preventing exploitation of the individual.

The consequence of disobedience is destruction of the land, which God so cares for that he will heal it in the absence of its unfaithful inhabitants:

> If in spite of this you do not listen to me and still defy me . . . I will make your cities desolate and destroy your sanctuaries . . . your land shall be desolate and your cities heaps of rubble. Then, all the time that it lies desolate, while you are in exile in the land of your enemies, your land shall enjoy its sabbaths to the full.
>
> (Lev. 26: 27–35)

If in Israel today there is only a handful of agricultural collectives which observe the 'sabbath of land' in its biblical and rabbinic sense, the biblical text has undoubtedly influenced the country's scientists and agronomists to question the intensive agriculture favoured in the early years of the State and to give high priority to conservation of land resources.

CUTTING DOWN FRUIT TREES

> When you are at war, and lay siege to a city . . . do not destroy its trees by taking the axe to them, for they provide you with food.
>
> (Deut. 20: 19)

In its biblical context this is a counsel of prudence rather than a principle of conservation; the Israelites are enjoined to use only 'non-productive', that is, non-fruit-bearing trees, for their siege works.

In rabbinic teaching, however, the verse has become the *locus classicus* for conserving all that has been created, so that the very phrase *bal tashchit* (literally 'not to destroy') is inculcated into small children to teach them not to destroy or waste even those things they do not need. In an account of the commandments specially written for his son, Rabbi Aaron Halevi of Barcelona (c. 1300) sums up the purpose of this one as follows:

> This is meant to ingrain in us the love of that which is good and beneficial and to cleave to it; by this means good will imbue our souls and we will keep far from everything evil or destructive. This is the way of the devout and those of good deeds – they love peace, rejoice in that which benefits people and brings them to Torah; they never destroy even a grain of mustard, and are upset at any destruction they see. If only they can save anything from being spoilt they spare no effort to do so.
>
> (*Sefer Ha-Hinnukh* Mitzvah 529)

In view of the great esteem in which the rabbis held the Temple service, it is remarkable that they forbade the use of olive and fig wood on the altar, but the destruction of such trees would frustrate settlement of the land.

LIMITATION OF GRAZING RIGHTS

The Mishnah rules: 'One may not raise small cattle [sheep, goats, etc.] in the Land of Israel, but one may do so in Syria or in the uninhabited parts of the land of Israel' (M. *Bava Qama* 7: 7). There is evidence of similar restrictions from as early as the third century BCE.

The Mishnah itself does not provide a rationale for the law. Later rabbis suggest (a) that its primary purpose is to prevent the 'robbery' of crops by roaming animals, and (b) that its objective is to encourage settlement in the Land. This latter reason is based on the premise that the raising of sheep and goats is inimical to the cultivation of crops, and reflects the ancient rivalry between nomad and farmer; at the same time it poses the question considered by modern ecologists of whether animal husbandry is an efficient way of producing food.[15]

AGRICULTURAL FESTIVALS

The concept of 'promised land' is an assertion that the consummation of social and national life depends on harmony with the land.

The biblical pilgrim festivals all celebrate the Land and its crops, though they are also given historical and spiritual meanings. Through the joyful collective experience of these festivals the people learned to cherish the Land and their relationship, through God's commandments, with it; the sense of joy was heightened through fulfilment of the divine commandments to share the bounty of the land with 'the Levite, the stranger, the orphan and the widow' (Deut. 16: 11 and elsewhere).

Specific environmental laws

Several aspects of environmental pollution are dealt with in traditional *halakhah*. Although the classical sources were composed in situations very different from those of the present, the law has been, and is, in a continuous state of development. In addition, in any case the basic principles are clearly relevant to contemporary situations.

WASTE DISPOSAL

Arising from Deuteronomy 23: 13, 14, *halakhah* insists that refuse be removed 'outside the camp', that is, collected in a location where it will not reduce the quality of life. The Talmud and Codes extend this concept to the general prohibition of the dumping of refuse or garbage where it may interfere with the environment or with crops.

It would be anachronistic to seek in the earlier sources the concept of waste disposal as threatening the total balance of nature or the climate. However, if the rabbis forbade the growing of kitchen gardens and orchards around Jerusalem on the grounds that the manuring would degrade the local environment (B. *Bava Qama* 82b), one need have no doubt that they would have been deeply concerned at the large-scale environmental degradation caused by traditional mining operations, the burning of fossil fuels and the like. We cannot know for sure how they would have responded had they been faced by the problem of disposal of nuclear wastes, but we need not doubt that their approach would have been firm and judicious.

Smell (see also the following section) is regarded in *halakhah* as a particular nuisance, hence there are rules regarding the siting not only of lavatories but also of odoriferous commercial operations such as tanneries.[16] Certainly, rabbinic law accords priority to environmental over purely commercial considerations.

ATMOSPHERIC POLLUTION AND SMOKE

Like smell, atmospheric pollution and smoke are placed by the rabbis within the category of indirect damage, since their effects are produced at a distance. They are nevertheless unequivocally forbidden.

The Mishnah (M. *Bava Batra* Ch. 2) bans the siting of a threshing floor within fifty cubits of a residential area, since the flying particles set in motion by the threshing process would diminish the quality of the air.

Likewise, the second-century rabbi Nathan (T. *Bava Batra* 1: 7) ruled that a furnace might not be sited within fifty cubits of a residential area because of the effect of its smoke on the atmosphere; the fifty cubit limit was subsequently extended by the Gaonim to whatever the distance necessary to prevent smoke causing eye irritation or general annoyance.[17]

The Hazards Prevention Law, passed by the Israeli Knesset on 23 March 1961, contains the following provisions:

#3 No person shall create a strong or unreasonable smell, of whatever origin, if it disturbs or is likely to disturb a person nearby or passerby.

#4a No person shall create strong or unreasonable pollution of the air, of whatever origin, if it disturbs or is likely to disturb a person nearby or passerby.

The subjectivity of 'reasonable' in this context is apparent. Meir Sichel (1985: 25–43), in a recent study on the ecological problems that arise from the use of energy resources for power stations to manufacture electricity, and from various types of industrial and domestic consumption such as cooking, heating and lighting, has drawn on the resources of traditional Jewish law in an attempt to define more precisely what should be regarded as 'reasonable'. Citing rabbinic Responsa from an 800-year period, he concludes that *halakhah* is even more insistent on individual rights than the civil law (of Israel), and that *halakhah* does not recognise 'prior rights' of a defendant who claims that he had established a right to produce the annoyance or pollutant before the plaintiff appeared on the scene.

It seems to me that in an exercise such as Sichel's, there is no difficulty in applying traditional law to the contemporary context with regard to priority of rights, and also in clarifying the relationship between public and private rights. However, it is less clear that one can achieve a satisfactory definition of 'reasonable', since ideas of what is acceptable vary not only from person to person but also in accordance with changing scientific understanding of the nature of the damage caused by smells and smoke – including the 'invisible' hazards of germs and radiation unknown to earlier generations.

WATER POLLUTION

Several laws were instituted by the rabbis to safeguard the freedom from pollution (as well as the fair distribution) of water. A typical early source:

> If one is digging out caves for the public he may wash his hands, face and feet; but if his feet are dirty with mud or excrement it is forbidden.

> [If he is digging] a well or a ditch [for drinking water], then [whether his feet are clean or dirty] he may not wash them.
>
> (T. *Bava Metzia* 11: 31, ed. Zuckermandel)

Pregnant with possibilities for application to contemporary life is the principle that one may claim damages or obtain an appropriate injunction to remove the nuisance where the purity of one's water supply is endangered by a neighbour's drainage or similar works. It is significant that the Gaonim here also rejected the talmudic distance limit in favour of a broad interpretation of the law to cover damage irrespective of distance (cited in *Shulhan Arukh: Hoshen Mishpat* 155: 21).

NOISE

Rabbinic law on noise pollution offers a fascinating instance of balance of priorities. The Mishnah lays down that in a residential area neighbours have the right to object to the opening of a shop or similar enterprise on the grounds that the noise would disturb their tranquillity. It is permitted, however, to open a school for Torah notwithstanding the noise of children, for education has priority. Later authorities discuss the limit of noise which has to be tolerated in the interest of education,[18] and whether other forms of religious activity might have similar priority to the opening of a school (*Shulhan Arukh: Hoshen Mishpat* 156: 3).

BEAUTY

Much could be said of the rabbinic appreciation of beauty in general. Here we concern ourselves only with legislation explicitly intended to enhance the environment, and we discover that it is rooted in the biblical law of the Levitical cities:

> Tell the Israelites to set aside towns in their patrimony as homes for the Levites, and give them also the common land surrounding the towns. They shall live in the towns, and keep their beasts, their herds, and all their livestock on the common land. The land of the towns which you give the Levites shall extend from the centre of the town outwards for a

> thousand cubits in each direction. Starting from the town the eastern boundary shall measure two thousand cubits, the southern two thousand, the western two thousand, and the northern two thousand, with the town in the centre. They shall have this as the common land adjoining their towns.
>
> (Num. 35: 2–5)

As this passage is understood by the rabbis, there was to be a double surround to each town, first a 'green belt' of a thousand cubits, then a two thousand cubit wide belt for 'fields and vineyards'. While some maintained that the thousand cubit band was for pasture, Rashi (on B. *Sota* 22b) explains that it was not for use, but 'for the beauty of the town, to give it space' – a concept reflected in Maimonides' interpretation of the talmudic rules on the distancing of trees from residences (see *Mishneh Torah*: *Shekhenim* ch. 10).

The rabbis debate whether this form of 'town planning' ought to be extended to non-Levitical towns, at least in the land of Israel, designated by Jeremiah (3: 19) and Ezekiel (20: 6,15) 'the beautiful land'.

The rabbinic appreciation of beauty in nature is highlighted in the blessing they set to be recited when one sees the first blossoms in spring (see p. 102).

Sample ethical problems relating to conservation

ANIMAL VERSUS HUMAN LIFE

Judaism consistently values human life more than animal life. One should not risk one's life to save an animal; for instance, if one is driving a car and a dog runs into the road, it would be wrong to swerve – endangering one's own or someone else's life – to save the dog.

But is it right to take a human life, e.g. that of a poacher, to save not an individual animal but an endangered species? I can find nothing in Jewish sources to support killing poachers in any circumstances other than those in which they directly threaten human life. If it be argued that the extinction of a species would threaten human life because it would upset the balance of nature, it is still unlikely that Jewish law would countenance homicide to avoid an indirect and uncertain threat of this nature.

Even if homicide were justified in such circumstances, how many human lives is a single species worth? How far down the evolutionary scale would such a principle be applied? After all, the argument about upsetting the balance of nature applies equally to microscopic species and to large cuddly-looking vertebrates like the giant panda, and to plants as much as to animals.

Judaism, true to the hierarchical principle of creation (see Hierarchy in creation above), consistently values human life more than that of other living things, but at the same time stresses the special responsibility of human beings to 'work on and look after' the created order (Gen. 2: 15 – see section: Stewardship or domination? above).

PROCREATION VERSUS POPULATION CONTROL

The question of birth control (including abortion) in Judaism is too complex to deal with here, but there is universal agreement that at least some forms of birth control are permissible where a potential mother's life is in danger, and that abortion is not only permissible but mandatory, up to full term, to save the mother's life.[19] Significant is the value system which insists that, even though contraception may be morally questionable, it is preferable to abstinence where danger to life would be involved through normal sexual relations within a marriage.

What happens where economic considerations rather than life danger come into play? Here we must distinguish between (a) personal economic difficulties, and (b) circumstances of 'famine in the world', where economic hardship is general. On the whole, *halakhah* places the basic duty of procreation above personal economic hardship. But what about general economic hardship, which can arise through (a) local or temporary famine, and (b) the upward pressure of population on finite world resources?

The former situation was in the mind of the third-century Palestinian sage, Resh Lakish, when he ruled: 'It is forbidden for a man to engage in sexual intercourse in years of famine' (B. *Taanit* 11a). Although the ruling of Resh Lakish was adopted by the codes (*Shulhan Arukh: Orach Hayyim* 240: 12 and 574: 4), its application was restricted to those who already have children, and the decision between abstinence and contraception is less clear here than where there is a direct hazard to life.

Upward pressure of population on world resources is a concept unknown to the classical sources of the Jewish religion, and not indeed clearly understood by anyone before Malthus. As Feldman remarks:

> It must be repeated here that the 'population explosion' has nothing to do with the Responsa, and vice versa. The Rabbis were issuing their analyses and their replies to a specific couple with a specific query. These couples were never in a situation where they might aggravate a world problem; on the contrary, the Jewish community was very often in a position of seeking to replenish its depleted ranks after pogrom or exile.
>
> (*Marital Relations, Birth Control and Abortion in Jewish Law*, p. 304)

Feldman goes on to say 'It would be just as reckless to overbreed as to refrain from procreation'. Although I am not aware of any explicit traditional rabbinic source for this, I certainly know of none to the contrary. Indeed, as the duty of procreation is expressed in Genesis in the words 'be fruitful and multiply and fill the earth', it is not unreasonable to suggest that 'fill' be taken as 'reach the maximum population sustainable at an acceptable standard of living but do not exceed it'. In like manner the rabbis (B. *Yevamot* 62a) utilise Isaiah's (45: 18) phrase 'God made the earth . . . no empty void, but made it for a place to dwell in', to define the minimum requirement for procreation – a requirement, namely one son and one daughter, which does not increase population.

Of course, there is room for local variation among populations. Although as a general rule governments nowadays should discourage population growth, there are instances of thinly populated areas or of small ethnic groups whose survival is threatened, where some population growth might be acceptable even from the global perspective.

NUCLEAR, FOSSIL FUEL, SOLAR ENERGY

Can religious sources offer guidance on the choice between nuclear and fossil, and other energy sources?

It seems to me that they can have very little to say and that – especially in view of the extravagant views expressed by some religious leaders – it is vitally important to understand why their potential contribution to current debate is so small.

The choice among energy sources rests on the following parameters:

1. Cost effectiveness
2. Environmental damage caused by production
3. Operational hazards
4. Clean disposal of waste products
5. Long-term environmental sustainability.

Let us consider these parameters. Cost effectiveness cannot be established without weighing the other factors. There is no point, however, at which religious considerations apply in establishing whether a particular combination of nuclear reactor plus safety plus storage of waste, and so on, will cost more or less than alternative 'packages' for energy production.

It is equally clear that religious considerations have no part to play in assessing environmental damage caused by production, operational hazards, whether waste products can be cleanly disposed of, or what is the long-term environmental sustainability of a method of energy production. These are all technical matters, demanding painstaking research and hard evidence, and they have nothing to do with theology.

The religions would have something to say about overall strategy. For instance, a religious viewpoint would suggest that scientists pay more attention to finding out how to use less energy to meet demands for goods than they do to finding out how to produce more energy; religions, after all, teach prudence, and should caution scientists against being carried away by the excitement of their own discoveries – one does not develop nuclear energy because it is an exciting concept, but because it is prudent to do so.

Religious leaders should take great care not to object to nuclear energy as a matter of principle. There is no spiritual value in using coal or even direct solar energy rather than nuclear energy; the costs and benefits of each, including their environmental costs and benefits, must be assessed objectively and dispassionately. Much hurt arises when the religious 'demonise' those of whom they disapprove, and in the name of love generate hatred against people who seek to bring benefit to humanity; they can be far more helpful when they ask the sort of questions suggested by their insight into our relationship with creation, and insist on adequate research being done before resources are committed to projects which may turn out to be harmful.

GLOBAL WARMING

A very similar analysis could be made of the problems relating to global warming – problems of which scientists have been aware since Arrhenius in the late nineteenth century, though only recently have pressure groups developed and governments become alarmed. The fact is that, at present, no-one knows the extent, if any, to which global temperatures have risen as a result of the rise in atmospheric carbon dioxide from 290 parts per million in 1880 to 352 parts per million in 1989. Similarly, no-one knows what would be the overall effects of the projected doubling of atmospheric carbon dioxide by the middle of next century (I leave aside the question of other greenhouse gases). Some consequences, indeed, may be beneficial, such as greater productivity of plants in an atmosphere with more carbon dioxide. Unfortunately, neither the techniques of mathematical modelling used to make the projections, nor the base of global observations at 500 kilometre intervals, can yield firm results.

So how can a government decide whether to spend hundreds of billions of dollars on reducing atmospheric carbon dioxide, and vast sums in aiding third world countries to avoid developing along 'greenhouse' lines, when the draconian measures required greatly limit personal freedom and much of the expenditure might be better diverted to building hospitals, improving education and the like?

Essential steps, including better research, must be initiated, but it would be a lack of wisdom to rush into the most extreme measures demanded. From our point of view, however, it is clear that the decisions must be rooted in prudence, rather than in any specifically religious value (of course, all religions commend prudence).

WHO PAYS THE PIPER?

Our observations on the response to the possibility of global warming raised the question of paying for conservation. The dilemmas involved in this are exceedingly complex. Should rich nations pay to 'clean up' the technology of poorer nations (e.g. Western Europe pay for Eastern Europe)? Should governments distort the free market by subsidising lead-free petrol and other 'environment-friendly' commodities? How does one assess environmental efficiency and social costs, and how should such costs be allocated between taxpayer, customer and manufacturer? Such questions are too complex, and on the whole too new, for us to find exact analogies in our sources, even though certain broad principles, such as the need for market intervention for social purposes, are well attested.

DIRECTED EVOLUTION

After writing about the progress from physical evolution through biological evolution to cultural evolution, Edward Rubinstein continues:

> Henceforth, life no longer evolves solely through chance mutation. Humankind has begun to modify evolution, to bring about nonrandom, deliberate changes in DNA that alter living assemblies and create assemblies that did not exist before.
>
> The messengers of directed evolution are human beings. Their messages, expressed in the language and methods of molecular biology, genetics and medicine and in moral precepts, express their awareness of human imperfections and reflect the values and aspirations of their species.
>
> ('Stages of Evolution and their Messengers', *Scientific American*, June 1989, p. 104)

These words indicate the area where Judaism most needs to adjust itself to contemporary reality – the area in which modern knowledge sets us most apart from those who formed our religious traditions. Religion as we know it has come into being only since the Neolithic Revolution, and thus presupposes some technology,[20] some mastery of nature. Our traditional sources seem to assume that the broad situation of humanity is static, and this is now seen to be an illusion.

All at once there is the prospect, alarming to some yet challenging to others, that we can set the direction of future development for all creatures in our world. The ethics committees of our hospitals and medical schools are forced to take decisions; although the religions take part – and Judaism has a distinctive contribution to make to medical ethics – it has yet to be shown that traditional sources can be brought to bear other than in the vaguest way ('we uphold the sanctity of life') on the problems raised even by currently available genetic engineering.

Will religions, as so often in the past, obstruct the development of science? They need not. Jewish religious views have ranged from Isaac Abravanel, who opposed in principle the development of technology,[21] to Abraham bar Hiyya, who in the twelfth century played a major role in the transmission of Graeco-Arab science to the West. If Judaism (or any other religion) is to contribute towards conservation it will need to be in the spirit of bar Hiyya, through support for good science, rather than through idealisation of the 'simple life' in the spirit of Abravanel.

Conclusion – religion and conservation

There is no doubt that Judaism, along with other religions, has resources which can be used to encourage people in the proper management of Planet Earth. We will now review the interaction of religion with conservation, with special reference to the sources cited.

1. We saw in the section entitled Goodness of the physical world how Judaism interprets the created world, with its balanced biodiverse ecology, as a 'testimony to God', with humankind at the pinnacle holding special responsibility for its maintenance and preservation. Certainly, this attitude is more conducive to an interest in conservation than would be emphasis on the centrality of the 'next world', on the spirit versus the body, or on the 'inferior' or 'illusionary' nature of the material world.
2. One of the priorities of conservation at the present time is to control population so as not to exceed resources. Although

Judaism stresses the duty of procreation, we learned that it offers the prospect of a constructive approach to population planning, including some role for both contraception and abortion (see Procreation versus population control, above).

3. We have noted several specific areas in which Judaism has developed laws or policies significant for conservation. Prime among them were the laws regulating the relationship between people and land, for which the 'chosen people' in the 'promised land' is the model (see Land and the people – a paradigm). Care of animals (see Concern for animals), waste disposal, atmospheric and water pollution, noise, and beauty of the environment (see Specific environmental laws) were also treated in the classical sources. It would be neither possible nor fully adequate to take legislation straight from these sources; but it is certainly possible to work in continuity with them, bearing in mind the radically new awareness of the need for conserving the world and its resources as a whole.
4. Religions, Judaism included, discourage the pursuit of personal wealth. While in some instances this may be beneficial to the environment – if people want fewer cars and fewer books there will be fewer harmful emissions and fewer forests will be chopped down – there are also many ways in which poverty harms the environment: for instance, less research and development means that such technology as remains (presumably for hospitals and other welfare projects) will be less efficient and the problems of environmental pollution less effectively addressed. It is a moot point whether lower technologies generate less pollution *pro rata* than advanced ones.
5. Some religions remain strongly committed to evangelistic or conversionist aims which inhibit co-operation with people of other religions. Judaism is not currently in an actively missionary phase; some would say that it is unduly introspective, and needs to proclaim its values in a more universal context. All religions, however, must desist from ideological conflicts and espouse dialogue; conservation cannot be effective without global co-operation.
6. Mere information can motivate, as when someone who perceives a lion ready to pounce reacts swiftly. If ecological disaster were as clearly perceived as a crouching lion, ideological motivation would be unnecessary. It is better that religions

support conservation than oppose it, but the world would be safer if people would act on the basis of rational collective self-preservation rather than on the basis of confused and uncontrollable ideologies.

7. Several times, particularly in discussing energy sources (see Nuclear, fossil fuel, solar energy section) and in the global warming section, we had to stress the need to distinguish between technological and value judgements. Whether or not nuclear reactors should be built must depend on a careful, dispassionate assessment of their hazards; shrill condemnation of the 'hubris of modern technology' merely hinders judgement, though it is right and proper that religious values be considered when an informed choice is made.

   Of course, the same need for objective assessment before value judgements are made applies to all other major conservation questions, such as how to reverse deforestation, control the greenhouse effect, restore the ozone layer, and so on.

   This is not a recipe for moral paralysis, but a way to avoid moral arbitrariness.

8. Towards the end of the section on directed evolution we noted a characteristic religious ambivalence towards science. In the interests of conservation it is essential that the 'pro-science' attitude of Abraham bar Hiyya, Maimonides and others be encouraged. The folly of 'simple life' advocates must be resisted. For a start, the present world population could not be supported if we were to revert to the simple life. Moreover, who would wish to do without sanitation, communications, electric light, books, travel, medical services and all those other benefits of 'complex' civilisation? The small population which would survive the 'return to Eden' would live a very dull and insecure life.

   There is indeed a question as to what level of technology – simple, intermediate, advanced – is most appropriate in a given situation. We should not be surprised if scientific evidence indicates that in some situations simple technology is preferable to advanced, whether because of availability or skills and resources, or whether because of side effects such as pollution. Once again, the moral issue is straightforward (one should achieve the most satisfactory balance between people's wants and the conservation of nature), but the decision has to be

A MODEL JEWISH STATEMENT ON NATURE

ONE *Creation is good; it reflects the glory of its creator*

'God saw everything he had made, and indeed it was very good' (Genesis 1: 31). Judaism affirms life, and with it the creation as a whole.

TWO *Biodiversity, the rich variety of nature, is to be cherished*

In Genesis 1, everything is said to be created 'according to its kind'. In the story of the Flood, Noah has to conserve in the ark male and female of every species of animal, so that it may subsequently procreate.

THREE *Living things range from lower to higher, with humankind at the top*

Genesis 1 depicts a process of creation of order out of the primeval chaos. The web of life encompasses all, but human beings – both male and female (Genesis 1: 27), 'in the image of God' – stand at the apex of this structure.

FOUR *Human beings are responsible for the active maintenance of all life*

Setting people at the top of the hierarchy of creation places them in a special position of responsibility towards nature. Adam is placed in the garden of Eden 'to till it and to preserve it' (Genesis 2: 15), and to 'name' (that implies, understand) the animals.

FIVE *Land and people depend on each other*

The Bible is the story of the chosen people and the chosen land. The prosperity of the land depends on the people's obedience to God's covenant: 'If you pay heed to the commandments which I give you this day, and love the Lord your God and serve him with all your heart and soul, then I will send rain for your land in season . . .' (Deuteronomy 11: 13–17). In the contemporary global situation, this means that conservation of the planet depends on (a) the social justice and moral integrity of its people, and (b) a caring, even loving, attitude to land, with effective regulation of its use.

SIX *Respect creation – do not waste or destroy*

Bal tashchit ('not to destroy – see Deuteronomy 20: 19) is the Hebrew phrase on which the rabbis base the call to respect and conserve all that has been created.

(Norman Solomon, in Rose 1992, p. 21.
The statement has received the endorsement
of Orthodox, Conservative and Reform rabbis.)

> based on sound technical and scientific evidence.
> If science has got us into a mess (which I would dispute) the way out is not *no* science but *better* science, and science performed with a sense of moral responsibility.

Finally, let us note that Judaism, like other religions, has a vital role to play in eradicating those evils and promoting those values in society without which no conservation policies can be effective. The single greatest evil is official corruption, frequently rife in precisely those countries where conservation measures must be carried out. Next in line is drug addiction, with its associated trade. Religions must combat these evils and at the same time work intelligently for peace, not only between nations but among religions themselves.

NOTES

1. Lichtenstein's paper was published (in Hebrew) in *Haggut* V, Religious Education Department of the Israel Ministry of Education: Jerusalem 5740/1980, pp. 101–108.
2. To the third-century Palestinian, Rabbi Abbahu, the *Midrash Bereshit Rabbah* 3: 9 attributes the statement that God 'created and destroyed worlds before he made this' – which is presumably his final, perfect design.
3. See David Ehrenfeld and Philip J. Bentley (1985) 'Judaism and the Practice of Stewardship', *Judaism* 34: 310–11.
4. Abraham Isaac Kook was born in Latvia and emigrated to Palestine in 1904, becoming Chief Rabbi of the Ashkenazi communities of Palestine when the office was instituted in 1921. A man of great piety and erudition, his numerous works are imbued with mysticism, and he emphasised the role of holiness in establishing the Jewish presence in the Holy Land. A selection of his writings translated into English is published under the title *Abraham Isaac Kook* in the series The Classics of Western Spirituality (Paulist Press: New York, 1978).
5. This is a traditional Jewish understanding of the text. Versions such as 'For ever is mercy built' (translation of the Jewish Publication Society of America, consonant with several English versions) are more grammatically sound.
6. I have taken the quotation from the texts on *Protection of Animals* published (in Hebrew) by the Israel Ministry of Justice in February 1976, but have been unable to check the original source. This publication of the Ministry of Justice together with its volume on

Protection of the Environment (July 1972) is an excellent resource for traditional texts on these subjects, having been compiled to assist those responsible for drafting legislation for the Knesset. The volumes were compiled by Dr Nahum Rakover, in his capacity as Adviser on Jewish Law to the Ministry of Justice.

7. In view of the ending of the verse this is a more appropriate translation of Hebrew *adam*, a generic term for humankind, than the sexist 'man'.
8. Heb. *mazzal* – literally 'constellation', but understood also as 'guardian angel'.
9. This is well explained in Chapter 8 of David Novak (1983) *The Image of the Non-Jew in Judaism* (Toronto Studies in Theology No. 14, New York and Toronto: Edwin Mellen Press).
10. In B. *Shabbat* 128b it is suggested that this principle is of biblical status (*d'oraita*).
11. See Schwartz (1982) and Bleich (1989) 237–250b for a review of the halakhic literature on vegetarianism.
12. In his Commentary *Baer Heitev* on *Shulhan Arukh: Orah Hayyim* Ch. 134. n. 3.
13. See note 6. He gives a wide range of references to the Responsa, many of which come from Renaissance Italy which provided most of the very few instances of Jews in pre-modern times engaging in hunting.
14. He implies that participating in hunting takes one out of the company of Torah scholars and into that of those who mock at religious values.
15. Some caution is needed here. The rabbis of the Talmud did not envisage vegetarianism, and did not ban the raising of large cattle in the Land. They assumed that meat would be eaten but tried to ensure that its production would not interfere with agriculture.
16. These matters are dealt with in the Talmud in the second chapter of *Bava Batra*. They are codified, with subsequent developments, in *Shulhan Arukh: Hoshen Mishpat* Ch. 145. Maimonides, in his philosophical work *Guide of the Perplexed* Book 3 Ch. 45, argues that the purpose of the incense in the Temple was to counteract the smell of the processing of the animal offerings.
17. A. Assaf (ed.) *Teshuvot ha-Gaonim* (Jerusalem: Darom, 5689/1929) p. 32. The Gaonim were the heads of the Babylonian academies after the completion of the Talmud; they occupy a major place in the development and transmission of rabbinic law.
18. Rashi on B. *Bava Batra* 21a. Nahmanides, in his commentary on the passage, hazards a guess that the permissible noise limit would be exceeded by a school of more than fifty pupils.
19. For a full treatment of these issues see David M. Feldman, *Marital Relations, Birth Control and Abortion in Jewish Law*. (Schocken Books: New York, 1974).

20. The ancients thought this had come from the gods, but Genesis 4: 20–22 polemically, if more accurately, credits humans with technological innovation.
21. See his commentary on Genesis 2. He taught that in the Messiah's time, as in Eden, we would wear no clothes, build no houses, abandon technology and have no government; in this he is more indebted to Seneca's 90th Epistle than to Jewish sources.

FURTHER READING

Bleich, J.D. (1989) *Contemporary Halakhic Problems*, vol. 3, New York, KTAV.

Ehrenfeld, David and Bentley, Philip J. (1985) 'Judaism and the Practice of Stewardship', *Judaism*, 34, pp. 310–11.

Freudenstein, Eric G. (1970) 'Ecology and the Jewish Tradition', *Judaism*, 19.

Gordis, Robert (1986) *Judaic Ethics for a Lawless World*, New York, Jewish Theological Seminary of America.

Kotler, David (1973) 'Jewish Ecology, Past and Present', *Jewish Observer*, May.

Pelcovitz, Ralph (1970) 'Ecology and Jewish Theology', *Jewish Life*, 37: 6, New York.

Press, Newtol (1985) 'Kosher Ecology', *Commentary*, 79: 2.

Rakover, Nahum, 'Pollution of the Environment in Jewish Law', in the Decennial Book (1973–1982) of the *Encyclopedia Judaica*, Jerusalem.

Rose, Aubrey (ed.) (1992) *Judaism and Ecology*, London, Cassell.

Schwartz, Richard (1982) *Judaism and Vegetarianism*, Smithtown, New York, Exposition Press.

Shochet, Elijah J. (1984) *Animal Life in Jewish Tradition: Attitudes and Relationships*, New York.

Sichel, Meir (1985) 'Air Pollution – Smoke and Odour Damage', *Jewish Law Annual*, V.

Solomon, Norman (1991) *Judaism and World Religion*, Basingstoke, Macmillan, Ch. 2.

6. Sikhism

Kanwaljit Kaur-Singh

Sikhism, one of the youngest religions, was founded by Guru Nanak, who was born in 1469 CE. He was followed by nine living Gurūs, and the tenth Gurū, Gobind Singh, declared Gurū Granth Sāhib, the Sikh scripture, to be the Gurū after his death. The teachings contained in the Gurū Granth Sāhib emphasise the Oneness of God, who is the creator of everything known and unknown; God is transcendent as well as immanent. The universe was, and is still, being created at the Creator's (God's) will. Human life is the apex of creation – the final stage and a starting point for God-realisation through service to humanity and sharing of responsibilities.

Nature

The Sikh Gurūs regarded nature as the manifestation and abode of God. Out of absolute being, God created nature, the indwelling spirit of the creation.

> God created himself and assumed a Name,
> Second besides himself, he created Nature,
> Seated in Nature, he watches with delight
> what he creates.[1]

(Gurū Granth Sāhib p. 463)

The spirit of God is continuously present in nature. Nature is in constant dependence upon his will. God himself transcends the world of things and does not depend on nature. God controls nature – his creation – as a king controls his kingdom:

> Nature is his throne, created for himself.
> From here he dispenses justice in the light of Truth.

Sikhism proclaims the glory of God in nature:

> In Nature we see God,
> in Nature we hear his speech;
> Nature inspires devotional reveries.
> In Nature is the essence of joy and peace.
> Earth, sky, nether regions comprise Nature.
> The whole creation is an embodiment of Nature.
> Air, water, fire, earth, dust are all parts of Nature,
> the Omnipotent Creator commands, observes and
> pervades Nature.
>
> (Gurū Granth Sāhib p. 464)

The expanse of nature is unlimited and the creator alone knows its wealth and volume:

> Nature is omnipresent and is beyond value.
> Even if one were to know its value,
> One would become mute while trying to describe it.
>
> (Gurū Granth Sāhib p. 84)

The Sikh Gurūs frequently drew lessons from the objects of nature. Apart from its apparent beauty, nature has a suggestiveness for them. They find in it love, sympathy, light, joy and peace. Gurūs see the hand of God in the symmetry, contours and splendour of natural objects; the hills, the valleys, the flowers and fruits, with their blossoms and fragrance, fill them with wonder and joy. Guru Nanak often tells us what we have to learn from objects of nature.

> The *simal* tree is huge and straight,
> But if one comes to it with hope of gain
> what will one get and whither turn?
> Its fruit is without taste,
> Its flowers have no fragrance

Its leaves are of no use.
O Nanak, humility and sweetness
are the essence of virtue and goodness.

(Gurū Granth Sāhib p. 470)

One of Guru Nanak's important poetic compositions on nature is *Bārah-māhā* – the song of the twelve months. In this calendar he describes the sorrows and joys of the pilgrim-soul, who, like a love-lorn woman, goes through the periods of storm and calm of separation and hope of union. Nature intensifies the agony of separation, particularly in the extremes of hot or cold weather. The moods of the month have both positive and negative effects on the soul's journey to its destination. The hymn describes the phenomenon of nature, its effects on the human mind and the means of union with God.

Guru Nanak saw the hand of God in the scenes of nature, and also nature singing the praises of God in its own way. The Gurū describes the scene of nature adoring the Almighty:

The firmament is thy salver,
The sun and moon thy lamps,
The galaxy of stars as pearls strewn.
A mountain of sandal is thy joss-stick.
Breezes that blow thy fan.
All the woods and vegetation
All the flowers that bloom
Take their colours from thy light.

(Gurū Granth Sāhib p. 663)

Sikh Gurūs, in advising Sikhs to pray and meditate in the early hours of the morning, used beautiful examples from nature to underline the tranquillity of this time. Guru Amar Das, the third Gurū, wrote:

At dawn God orders all the elements of nature
(light, sound, water, air, fragrance, solitude, peace)
to bless all seekers now and help them in their
union with God.

(Gurū Granth Sāhib p. 1285)

Guru Arjan Dev, the fifth Gurū, wrote:

When the birds chirp at dawn, the sun's rays are struggling
to pierce through the blanket of darkness
creating numerous wonderful colours in water, streams
rivers, oceans. The petals of flowers bathed in dew.

(Gurū Granth Sāhib p. 319)

Unity of God

Guru Nanak proclaimed that there is but one God, who is above birth and death, who has existed from all eternity and by whose power this universe had been created by a simple act of his will. He said, 'Thou alone art, The one True Lord, Truth is Thy Law and Rule' (Gurū Granth Sāhib p. 463).

The Mūl Mantra, the opening verse of the Gurū Granth Sāhib, defines God as *Karatā Purakh* (the creator):

There is one God,
The sole Supreme Being of eternal manifestation;
Creator, Immanent Reality, Without fear,
Without rancour, Timeless Form, Unincarnated,
Self Existent.

God, the creator and master of all forms in the universe, is responsible for all modes of nature and all elements in the world. The Gurū says:

Humans, trees, holy places,
coasts, clouds, fields
islands, continents, universes,
spheres, and solar systems,
life forms – egg-born, womb-born, earth-born, sweat-born –
only God knows their existence:
in oceans, mountains, everywhere.
Nanak says God created them and
God takes care of them all.

(Gurū Granth Sāhib p. 467)

The cosmic process

Before creation and the cosmic process, God was in abstract meditation. This state of his is known as *śūnyā samādhi* – state of contemplation of the void. Guru Nanak wrote:

> For countless ages, there was utter darkness,
> there was no earth and no sky, but the Infinite
> Lord's will alone was pervasive.
> There was neither day, nor night, neither sun nor moon,
> The creator was in abstract meditation.
> Existed then neither forms of creation, nor of speech,
> neither wind, nor water;
> Neither was creation nor disappearance nor transmigration.
> Then were not continents, neither regions,
> the seven seas, nor rivers with water flowing.
> Existed then neither heaven nor the mortal world
> nor the nether world.
> Then were not scriptures like Vedas and the Qur'ān, *Smṛti*s and *Śastra*s,
> Neither recitation of *Purāṇa*s, nor rise nor setting
> of sun.
> Unknowable himself, he was the source of all utterance;
> himself, the unknowable, unmanifested.
> As it pleased him, he created the Universe.

(Gurū Granth Sāhib p. 1035)

Thus the creator, from abstract form – *Nirguṇa* ('without attributes') – before he created the world, became manifest – *Saguṇa*. He diffused himself in nature and shaped the universe. Guru Nanak wrote:

> The firmament he spread without prop to support it.
> He made the planets, the solar systems and
> our universe in endless space.
> Above, below and around it,
> From absolute self he became manifest.

(Gurū Granth Sāhib p. 1037)

Limitlessness of the creation

The Gurū states that no prop or pillar supports this or any other planet in space, but that they stand, due to some divine law or laws unknown during his times. The Gurū questioned the then prevalent idea that the bull carried the earth on its horn:

How much is the load under which this Bull stands?
On what support does all this rest?
There are more worlds beyond this earth, more and more,
What power is that which supports their weight from underneath?
Countless are the created beings, their hues and names.
All the wise ones have attempted account of
these at one stretch,
Yet who may render the true account of all these?
How voluminous it would be?
Who may calculate God's might and the beautiful
forms created by it.
And of his blessings the extent?
All the endless expanse of creation arose of one note,
Giving rise to millions of streams.
How may I compute and express God's might?

(Gurū Granth Sāhib p. 3)

The passage illustrates that beyond the earth, in space, there are innumerable other worlds in the universe. Guru Nanak's contemporary world did not know about this, and instead regarded the sun, the moon and other stars as gods. Nanak wrote:

He has created millions of nether worlds and heavens;
men have given up the search in despair.
The Vedas too declare unanimously their helplessness.
Muslim scriptures declare the number of species –
eighteen thousand. Vain is such count; there is only one
essence, that God is limitless:
This infinity no one may measure or state.

(Gurū Granth Sāhib p. 5)

Gurū says that the whole universe is in motion, nothing is stationary. All these stars and other planets have extended over vast distances according to his divine law. 'Under his law, sun and moon keep on in motion; traversing millions of miles, they endlessly remain in motion' (Gurū Granth Sāhib p. 580).

In God's creation, there are innumerable galaxies, and in each galaxy there are many solar systems containing planets. These planets have their own civilisations, and each civilisation has its own prophets and creeds. In these millions of earths, there are millions of prophets working for the salvation of humanity. This universe is beyond our perception. As Guru Nanak put it, the creator alone knows it: 'God alone knows how great he is . . . The limit of his creation is not discerned' (Gurū Granth Sāhib p. 5).

Time of creation

There have been speculations about the time when the creator made this universe. Guru Nanak did not accept any theories put forward for the time of creation, and wrote in *Japjī Sāhib*:

> What were the hour and occasion,
> What the date and day,
> What the season and month,
> When creation began?
> The Pandits could not know the time,
> If so, they would have recorded it in their scriptures.
> The Qazis could not know the time,
> It would have been recorded in the Qur'ān.
> The Yogi knows not the date and day, season or month.
> The Creator who made the Universe, alone knows the answer.
>
> (Gurū Granth Sāhib p. 4)

Transcendent and immanent

Guru Nanak did not believe in an absentee God sitting idle. He saw the creator within his creation as well as outside it. The absolute transcendent power watched his creation, and his immanent spirit is always present in nature. He is thus the transcendent creator and the immanent basis of the whole creation, and he invests it with a unity which comes from constant dependence on him: 'God himself is the

Doer and the Deed, Himself the Creator and the Cause' (Gurū Granth Sāhib p. 1190).

Guru Nanak did not become so engrossed in the exclusive quest for transcendence that immanence is reduced to the category of illusoriness, which would make the search for temporal life hardly worth the effort. Sikhism believes that transcendence and immanence are inseparable for human experience. Therefore, the human mind and spirit, and the whole cosmic process are real and not illusory. Guru Angad, the second Gurū, wrote:

> Real are thy universes, regions and solar systems,
> Real are thy works and thy purposes.
> Hundreds of thousands, millions upon millions,
> call upon thee as the true Reality.
> All energies and forces are from that Reality.
> The laws of Nature, O God, are real:
> Those who worship the true Reality are real,
> And those who worship what is born and dies are most unreal.
>
> (Gurū Granth Sāhib p. 463)

The world is of two kinds; the world as God made it, and the world as made by human beings' own desires and attachments. If human beings become wrapped up in their desires and forget the spiritual path, then the world does become illusory.

Microcosmic and macrocosmic theory

According to Guru Nanak, 'What is there in the universe is also found in the human body, and he who seeks will find it' (Gurū Granth Sāhib p. 1041). The universe is the macrocosm and the body is the microcosm. The soul lives in the body and the higher soul lives in the universe. Since the soul and the higher soul are the same in essence, and the higher soul is reflected in the soul, similarly the universe is found in the body.

> In the body, God is present,
> the body is his temple.
> In the body is the place of pilgrimage
> of which I am the pilgrim.

In the body is the holy offering,
In the body the oblation.
He who pervades the universe
Also dwells in the body:
Who seeks shall find him there.

(Gurū Granth Sāhib p. 695)

The human body is considered the residence of Truth, and Truth can be attained through the medium of the body. The body is an epitome, a small index of the universe. Whatever exists in the universe also exists in the body of a human being. The physical processes of the universe and the biological processes in the human body are parallel. With this parallelism in mind, the moon, the sun and the stars are all located in the body. The same energy is in action, both in the universe and the human body. Guru Amar Das wrote:

None has been able to evaluate this body.
God has created it.
The pious control the body and meet him again,
There are innumerable things in this body:
The pious, after finding Truth, see them.

(Gurū Granth Sāhib p. 754)

The mortal world

The Gurūs very clearly explained the transitory nature of the whole world: 'God who has created the universe destroys it too' (Gurū Granth Sāhib p. 355). There is no basis for assuming the permanence of the world. God, who alone has created this limitless universe, has the power to destroy it. It came into existence with *Karatā Purakh*'s (Creator's) will, and will disappear when he wills it. Guru Nanak wrote:

The grave lies at the end of the road for all living things,
For the master and his disciples, for the prophets and for the kings.
The greatest of the earth are creatures of the moment that passes.
All creatures are mortal, thou alone art immortal.

(Gurū Granth Sāhib p. 143)

All living things are destined to come and go; death is the gift given to an organism at birth. The universe is also mortal. The Gurū says:

> Neither sun, moon nor the constellations
> Neither the seven continents, nor oceans,
> Nor the water, air and food (the sustenance) is immutable.
> Thou Lord, alone, art eternal, none but thou . . .
> God who builds, demolishes as well (in his will),
> there is no other apart from him. . . .
> Having destroyed, he recreates, and having recreated,
> he destroys as he wills. Having demolished, he rebuilds,
> and having rebuilt, he demolishes. Having filled the sea,
> he causes it to dry up and then fills it again.
> He alone, who is beyond all care and dependence,
> has the power to do so.
>
> (Gurū Granth Sāhib pp. 934–5)

Sustainer

God the creator and the destroyer is the only sustainer. All living things are sustained through his grace:

> If God wills, he may cause the tigers, hawks,
> kestrels and falcons to eat grass.
> He may likewise cause the grass-eating animals to eat meat.
> He thus can create life's pattern as he pleases.
> All creatures live by breathing, but he may sustain
> them even without it, if he so desires.
> Hence the True one sustains life as it pleases him.
>
> (Gurū Granth Sāhib p. 144)

Sikhism teaches that God looks after his creation, nothing is overlooked. Even creatures in rocks and stones are well-provided for. Birds who fly thousands of miles, leaving their young ones behind, know that they will be sustained and taught to fend for themselves. The creatures of nature lead their lives under God's command. Guru Nanak applauded their closeness to God:

If I were a doe living in the forest, eating grass
and leaves, with God's grace, I would find him.
If I were a cuckoo living in the mango tree,
contemplating and singing, God would reveal himself through his mercy.
If I were a female snake, dwelling in the ground, let God's
word be in my being, my dread would vanish.
Eternal God is found, light meets light.

(Gurū Granth Sāhib p. 157)

Centrality of human beings

Human beings, like everything else, owe their existence to the will of God. Human birth of course is a precious privilege: 'Blessed, blessed is the human birth, One attains it through virtue' (Gurū Granth Sāhib p. 575). The spirit that illumines the human soul, however, equally sustains all other beings.

All creatures have been given consciousness,
None has been created without it.
They follow the path according to their
understanding, and, judged in the same way,
they come and go.

(Gurū Granth Sāhib p. 24)

Everything, in fact, receives from the creator all the guidance it needs. In the animal world, the divine guidance takes the form of instinct. Instinct enables animals to make adjustments to their environment. The ducklings and chicks may have been hatched by the same hen but while the former fearlessly plunge into water, the latter shrink from it and keep to dry land. Each seems to know, instinctively, what it can do and what it cannot.

But it seems that God has endowed humanity with superior understanding and reason, with a capacity to exploit natural resources to its advantage and to improve its own life and environment. According to Sikhism, the individual soul has arrived at the human form after going through innumerable cycles of birth and death. The human life is an opportunity provided for development: 'All other forms of life are subject to you [human form], Your rule is on the earth' (Gurū Granth Sāhib p. 374). Human life is a focal point in the universe, the apex of creation – the final stage. One cannot attain salvation as an animal or as an inanimate object; only human life offers the grand opportunity for spiritual attainment. Out of millions and millions of creatures created by God, human beings alone are endowed with the intellect to understand the why and wherefore of existence. They alone have purpose and freedom of will, and a spark of responsibility. Guru Nanak portrayed human beings as living in the world and yearning for unity with the creator. Guru Nanak denounced the idea of renouncing society in search of the creator. The Gurū believed that human life can achieve transcendence only through living within the creation. He enunciated the positive path, which involved the collaboration of human beings in the task of humanity and in the direction of the cosmos. In this way alone, human beings can be exalted and can experience truth. Gurū says: 'Such is the divine play of the creator, that he has reflected the whole cosmos in the human body' (Gurū Granth Sāhib p. 117).

It is within an enlightened mind and heart that the cosmos is evaluated and the responsibility towards God's creation is comprehended. Sikhs are required to understand their duties and responsibilities, living within the world. 'A place in God's court can only be attained if we do service to others in this world.' Human beings enjoy the freedom of making decisions and are responsible for their actions. The freedom of actions is subject to the laws of nature; like everything else in this universe, the transgression of God's Laws, knowingly or unknowingly, causes pain and suffering. A Sikh is enjoined to live according to 'his will', and not to attempt to control nature. Sikh Gurūs warned against any notion of controlling nature. Gurū Granth Sāhib says, 'Nothing but God has power' (p. 83).

Human life is part and parcel of the ecosystem shared with other elements in the environment; that means that the conservation of the forest is also its own conservation. The destruction of the forest will, in the end, result in the destruction of human life. Human existence very much depends on the environment. Human beings, as rulers of the natural world order, have a duty to protect and save the environment from destruction. God is like a benevolent parent who has provided all beings with the means of sustenance; it is up to them to use their resources wisely. Life is compared to a game of chess or cards, where the individuals do not frame the rules or control the game. The cards or pieces are given to them and it is up to them to play the game well or badly, wisely or foolishly.

Sikhs and conservation

Sikhs, throughout their historical development, have always been sensitive to the importance of the environment, as it is a gift from God. As lovers of nature, Sikhs became by choice, professional farmers, horticulturists and conservationists of plant and animal resources. They participated wholeheartedly in the green revolution and the white (milk) revolution, and converted Panjab (a small area in relation to the size of India) into the breadbasket of India. In the creation of tree plantations in wetlands and wastelands, along roads and canals, in developing flower and fruit orchards, and in animal husbandry, the Sikhs have shown their ingenuity and prowess. Plant and animal conservation is a religious duty.[2] The Gurū says,

> Flower girl plucking petals, know in each
> petal abides life.
> The stone-image for which these petals
> are plucked is lifeless.
>
> (Gurū Granth Sāhib p. 479)

ATTITUDE TO MEAT-EATING

The Sikh Gurūs neither advocated nor forbade the eating of meat. The general directive of Guru Nanak with regard to food was, 'Do not take that food which has ill effects on health, causes pain or suffering to the body, or produces evil thoughts in the mind' (Gurū Granth Sāhib p. 16).

There is a close connection between the body and the mind, so that the food that we eat affects both of them. The Gurūs did not like the taboo on meat when more important things like control over desires or passion were ignored. They felt it far more important to kill the evil that pollutes the mind than to abstain from meat. Impurities of the mind should be removed first, before labelling some foods as pure and others as impure. This Sikh rejection of the concept of purity and pollution of food means that the eating of meat has less to do with religion than with personal choice. Guru Nanak actually criticised people who were scrupulous in matters of diet but indifferent to moral pollution. He said: 'They who give up meat and can't stand even its flavour, devour men in the darkness of night' (Gurū Granth Sāhib p. 1289). His view was emphasised and reiterated – he said again, 'It is strange that one born of the mother's and father's flesh, does not eat fish and meat'.

The Gurū's ultimate concern was to help men and women of all backgrounds to find the truth and, through it, spiritual liberation. Compared with this, disputes over food were trivial and only likely to distract attention from the things that really matter. Rebirth is not influenced by diet but by moral conduct, and good actions and service to humanity.[3] Vegetarianism by itself cannot confer spiritual merit or lead to the door of salvation. Spiritual achievement depends on religious discipline.

The unnecessary killing of vegetation or animals is the destroying of God's creation. 'If you say that god resides in all, Why do you kill a hen?' (Gurū Granth Sāhib p. 1350). The consumption of meat in Sikh homes is very small in comparison with that in homes in the western world. Sikhs use meat on special occasions such as feasts and parties, and special family gatherings; it is not a part of the daily diet. Sikhs also respect other people's dietary habits, and only vegetarian meals are served in the *laṅgar* (gurdwara kitchen).

Sikhs believe that there is life in everything we eat, whether that be vegetarian food or animal food – one type is not less pure than the other. Nevertheless, it also seems to be a law of nature that some animals are meat-eaters, whereas others live on plants and vegetation. This is all according to God's *hukam* (will). As already mentioned, Sikhs believe that if God wanted all animals to live on plants alone, he would have created them that way. Perhaps this is his way of controlling the species. The fact remains that Sikhs must not abuse his creation for selfish purposes, but use the resources with care and compassion.

CONCLUSION

As we know, environmental balance can be maintained only if the conservation designed by God is maintained, and this can be achieved only by adhering to ethical behaviour, as prescribed in the scriptures. The key principles of the Sikh faith are in tune with natural existence:

1. Pray to God – remember him and his authority.
2. Earn an honest living – do not take what does not belong to you, or more than you need.
3. Share with others who are less fortunate than you.

Conservation has concerned some Sikhs for a number of years. The best example is that of Bhagat Puran Singh of Pingalwara, Amritsar, who runs a home for the handicapped housing about 250 people. One of his concerns is conservation – not on a grand scale, but on issues such as how the water-levels in village wells are affected by the damming of rivers and by the introduction of irrigation schemes. Another such issue is the destruction of scrubland by farmers, which deprives poor villagers of an important source of fuel. He refuses grants of money from the government lest he find his freedom to criticise policies compromised. The Bhagat's work is a reminder that while governments may, quite properly, discuss the ozone layer and acid rain, for many of their voters the issues are more local and very immediate.[4]

In this respect Bhagat Puran Singh is following the lead given by the Sikh Gurūs, who themselves were sensitive to the need to conserve the environment, particularly vegetation and water. For water conservation, the Sikhs constructed tanks and made it holy work. They considered it a holy duty to subscribe to the periodical cleaning of tanks. The Sikh Gurūs developed colonies and gurdwaras along the banks of rivers, such as those constructed at Kartarpur by Guru Nanak, and at Paonta Sahib by Guru Gobind Singh. The Gurūs believed that water, the primal life which has made all the rest green, belongs to all.

NOTES

1. God is not a man or a woman, but a spirit that pervades the universe. The pronouns 'he' or 'him' for God are used because of the tradition of the English language, and not to denote the maleness of God.
2. Puri, Gopal Singh, 1989, 'Nature Consciousness in the Sikh Faith', in *World Religions in Education*, Shap Working Party/CRE, p. 32.

3. Sikhs do not venerate the cow as do Hindus, so beef is not taboo for the non-vegetarian Sikhs. However, Guru Gobind Singh prohibited the Sikhs from eating *ḥalāl* meat (meat which is prepared in the Muslim ritual way).
4. Cole, Owen, 1989, 'Conservation with reference to teaching Sikhism', in *World Religions in Education*, Shap Working Party/CRE, p. 36.

FURTHER READING

Kohli, S.S. (1961) *A Critical Study of the Adi Granth*, New Delhi, Punjabi Writers Cooperative Society.

Singh, Daljeet (1984) *The Sikh Ideology*, Delhi, Guru Nanak Foundation.

Singh, Manjit (1969) *Gurbani and Science Study*, Jullundur, Gur Das Kapur and sons.

Singh, Manmohan (1965) Translation of *Sri Guru Granth Sahib*, Amritsar, Shiromani Gurdwara Parbandhak Committee.

Singh, Tarlochan Singh (1969) *Guru Nanak's Religion*, Delhi, Guru Nanak Foundation.

7. Chinese Religions

Xinzhong Yao

Compared with other major religions in the world, the attitudes to nature in the Chinese religious tradition can be characterised as follows:

1. The emphasis is put on the cosmic order rather than on its creation.
2. Nature never stands isolated from humans, and the cosmic order is the basis and model of the social and moral order.
3. The highest religious ideal is to unify or identify humans with nature.

The prime concern of the ancient Chinese was to know the position of human beings in relation to the whole universe by observing the movement of the cosmos. Therefore, since the very beginning, the fate of humans has been connected closely with the law of the universe. Human beings are the microcosm of the macrocosm – their bodies, their lives and their morality can be traced to the original pattern of the latter. With this consideration as a starting point, several theories were put forward to justify why human beings should, and how they can, reach unification with nature, and why the harmonious state of nature must be the supreme reality of human beings.

Instead of using the concept of 'nature', the concepts of Heaven (*T'ien*) and earth and others have been widely used to refer to the cosmic environment outside human beings. Of them, *tao* and Heaven (*T'ien*) are two key terms which have a meaning similar to what we call 'nature', and upon which Taoism, Confucianism and popular religion built their respective religious systems.

Humanity follows *tao*

The modern Chinese term for 'nature' comes first from Lao Tzu's *Tao Te Ching*, where two characters, *zi ran*, are used to refer to the self and the original state of *tao*. One of the profound implications which we can find in this term expresses a religious acknowledgement of the foundation of the whole universe, and therefore this concept may be treated as equivalent to the Buddhist idea of *tathata*.

However, the term *zi ran* is not the nuclear concept in the *Tao Te Ching*. In fact, it is *tao* which was used by Lao Tzu (traditionally dated around the sixth century BCE) as his basic conception of the mysterious entity of Nature. He believed that there was one origin for all things, but that it defied any definition. In Chapter 25 of his book, he made it very clear that there is 'something undifferentiated and yet complete in Itself' and 'existing before Heaven and Earth', which must be the ultimate origin of the universe. If the existence is 'being', this 'something' before 'being' has to be 'non-being'. Just because it is non-being, human language is unable to designate it at all, and only when he was forced to give it a name did he call it the Great, or *tao*.

Every thing and every living being comes from this *tao*; the way of *tao* is also the way of life. Before the period of Spring and Autumn (around the eighth to the fifth centuries BCE), the emphasis had been put on the ways that the Supreme God (*Shang Ti* or *T'ien*) governs the universe. Lao Tzu, however, replaced this religious concept by a natural concept of *tao*. In the *Tao Te Ching*, *tao* is the origin of the whole universe, it is the mother of all things, but it is not like a personal God with will and emotion. *Tao* is a natural entity and *tao*'s 'creation' of the world is rather an evolutionary process of nature: '*Tao* begot one; one begot two; two begot three and three begot ten thousand things' (Chapter 42).

'The *tao* as the Order of Nature, which brought all things into existence and governed their very action' is also the universal principle or Law (Needham 1956: 37). In this sense, *tao* not only refers to the laws of nature according to which the movements of the universe – such as the phases of the moon, the changes of seasons, and growth and weathering of vegetation – proceed, but also points to the universal principle which governs human life and society. With these ideas in mind, Lao Tzu made *tao* the supreme reality which should be the model for human beings:

> Human beings follow the law of Earth. Earth follows the law of Heaven. Heaven follows the law of *tao* and *tao* follows its own nature.
>
> (Chapter 25)

Taoist masters also believe that *tao* has endowed each being with a distinctive nature which is called *te* (virtue or power), and the only way for a being to unite with the primordial *tao* is to cultivate its own nature. Chuang Tzu tried to give an outline of the True Person who exerted his *te* to the utmost. He said that the True Person is integrated in *tao*, so he neither feels glad when he is born into this world, nor feels unhappy when he departs. Only because he does not hold on to his self, can he take the whole universe as his home and freely travel between Heaven and Earth (Watson 1968: 78). Because of their emphasis on the primitive state of *tao*, Taoists are strongly against Confucian politics and social ethics, which are regarded as violations of the principle of *tao*. They propose an ideal for life: act naturally, that is, act with non-action and live by non-striving, because only by following the natural way are human beings able to return to their origin, and integrate themselves into the great nature.

This idea has played a dramatically important role in Taoist and popular religion in China, where 'entering the eternity by integrating with nature' is the constant hope and main purpose of religious activities. People can become immortal when, by acting naturally, they regain harmony with *tao*. Therefore, the question is not whether a person can or cannot become an immortal, but how he or she will become an immortal. In consequence, a number of methods emerged to cultivate one's *tao* and to absorb the essence of the cosmos (*chi*), such as living in the mountains, looking for the Isles of the Blessed, searching for the immortal herbs and practising alchemy.

Although varying in method, two principles underlie these religious activities. The first principle is: humanity and nature are the same. Because humans are a part of nature, and because nature is immortal and exists for ever, if we can realise that our true selves are nothing but nature itself, we will identify ourselves with nature and obtain immortality. The second principle is: *chi* pervades the whole cosmos, all living and non-living things. In its original state, *chi* is void, quiet and simple, but in humans this *chi* is active and disturbed by desires. What we have to do is to lead active *chi* to the quiet state of the cosmos by reducing desires. This practice is also called 'to return to one's beginning' – an innocent baby. Taoist masters repeatedly talk about the difference between the learning of knowledge and the practising of *tao*: when you are learning, you should add to your knowledge day by day; however, when you are practising, you must reduce day by day your knowledge, morality and desire, which you have obtained by learning in the social life and which are completely contrary to the nature of *tao*. Reducing and reducing until there is nothing inside you, you will reach *tao*. In *tao* you do nothing, but everything will be done. Having returned to the original state, your mind is empty, so you can easily grasp the truth of *tao*. Your heart is sincere, so you can receive nutrition from the cosmos. Through such cultivation you will enter eternity.

The unity of humans and *tao* is the harmony of self with the universe and is the only guarantee for a happy life. Following the unity is fortunate; opposing the unity is unfortunate. Keeping the unity, one will obtain an immortal life; losing the unity, life will perish (*Tao Te Ching* Chapter 25). Realisation of the unity in the microcosmic self and the macrocosmic universe, and keeping up its harmony and peace, are the ultimate goals of self-discipline.

Oneness of humanity and Heaven

If *tao* is the basis of human life in Taoism, then in Confucianism it is Heaven which provides an ideal for human beings, though these two concepts have been jointly used by Confucianism, Taoism and all other religions in China. Basically, there are two usages of Heaven (*T'ien*) in ancient Chinese literature. In the first sense, it was used as a personal concept meaning the 'Lord in Heaven', which is the highest god. In the second sense, it was used as a naturalistic term (sometimes in conjunction with 'earth'), meaning the natural universe or whole existing environment of human beings. In this chapter, Heaven is used mainly in its second sense, while its first meaning is dealt with in the volumes entitled *Worship* and *Picturing God* in this series.

The relationship between humanity and Heaven is a central topic in Chinese religion, philosophy and literature, where the dominant tendency is to reconcile rather than separate them: the Oneness of Heaven and humanity. There are two meanings of the oneness between humanity and Heaven. The first is their identification, that is, they are one in essence. The second is their reconciliation, that is, humans can, by their efforts, reach a harmonious state between themselves and Heaven.

Humans came from Heaven, the virtue of Heaven is also the virtue of human beings, and the *tao* of Heaven is exactly the *tao* of humanity. Confucius firmly believed that 'it is Heaven which endows the virtue in me' (*Analects*, 7: 23). Some Confucians tried to prove that the spiritual life is received from Heaven, while the physical life is endowed by earth. Mencius spent much time arguing that the principles of Heaven and earth exist in human nature. For people to realise fully what is in their hearts is for them to understand their own nature, and those who know their own nature will know Heaven. By 'retaining his heart' and 'nourishing his nature', they are serving Heaven (*Mencius*, see Lau 1970: 182). This theory has been one of the most influential theories in Confucianism, and from it, for quite a long period, Taoism and Buddhism also benefited.

Humans derive their rules, laws and morality from Heaven. *Li* (meaning rituals, rites, ceremony, propriety or moral laws) are founded in the regular procedure of Heaven, in the right phenomena of earth and in the proper actions of human beings (Munro 1969: 32). Hsun Tzu traced human morality to the cosmic principle and tried to unify humanity and heaven through *li*:

> It is through *Li* that Heaven and earth are harmonious and sun and moon are bright, that the four seasons are ordered and the stars are in their courses, that rivers flow, that things prosper, that love and hatred are tempered and joy and anger are in keeping.
>
> (*Hsun Tzu*, see de Bary et al. 1960: 109)

Heaven, earth and humanity are three main existences of the universe. Under the rule of the ancient Sage-kings, the people were in harmony with Heaven and earth. After that, humans lost their original identification with Heaven and earth, but not their ability to unite with them again. That is to say, it is possible for humans to return to their original position. One of the ways to do this is to cultivate one's morality, and to keep one's heart in *cheng* (sincerity), whereby this 'heart' can encompass the whole world. Therefore, in Confucianism, the religious ideal for an individual is not to become a god or an immortal, but to become a sage who stands with Heaven and earth to form a triad, and whose virtue, teachings and merits are the model for ten thousand generations. Starting from Mencius, Confucians strongly hold that everyone, because of his or her original nature and moral ability, can become a sage (in theory, at least, women are not excluded from the possibility of becoming sages). This is an effective principle which has been carried out both in social life and in religious belief, and which has also made a great impression on Taoism and Buddhism.

'All things are my companions'

Wu (things) in Chinese texts means either the whole creation in the cosmos, or, more specifically, all living creatures besides human beings. The relation between humans and things is another area where the attitude to nature is clearly represented.

Both humans and ten thousand things are products of the movement of the universe, and belong to the same 'family': 'Heaven and earth were born at the same time I was, and ten thousand things are one with me' (*Chuang Tzu*, see Watson 1968: 43). The world of things and the world of humans are intimately connected; therefore, any disturbance in the human realm affects also the realm of nature, and vice versa. In this interaction between these two worlds, Taoism emphasises human passiveness, that is, humans should always be in acceptance. However, Confucians put more importance on human activeness and on the effect which human life, especially the political life, would have on the world of things.

> When the human world is well governed and the people are at peace . . . the transforming influences of heaven and earth operate in a state of perfection and among the myriad things only the finest are produced. But when the human world is in disorder and the people become perverse . . . when the transforming influences of heaven and earth are rebellious, then the transforming influences of heaven and earth suffer injury, so that their [yin and yang's] ethers generate visitations and harm arises.
>
> (*Tung Chung-shu*, see Fung 1952–53 vol. II: 57)

Every existent has, and should have, its own position and value in the universe. Instead of depriving them of their value and even destroying them, it is our responsibility to protect and to help them in their proper course. More than two thousand years ago, the great Confucian, Hsun Tzu, talked about the preservation of the forest, animals and ecological environment:

> When shrubs and trees are in bloom and leaf, the axe must not enter the forest, people must not cut short the life of the trees or shrubs when young, nor stop their growth; when sea tortoises, water lizards, fish, turtles, eels, and sturgeons, are full of roe or have spawned, nets or poison must not enter the marshes or pools, people must not cut short the life of these water creatures when young nor stop their growth.
>
> (*Hsun Tzu*, see Dubs 1977: 138)

This prohibition is not only from sympathy with the creatures but also from the care for human prosperity. The life of creatures is connected with the life and prosperity of human beings. In special periods, hurting creatures will bring disasters. For example, spring is a time for growth, not for destruction, in which,

> If the emperor does not bestow favours and grant rewards, but rather allows great cutting, destroying and wounding, then he will be in danger. Should he not die, then the heir-apparent will be in danger, and some one of his family or consort will die, or else his eldest son will lose his life.
>
> (*Kuan Tzu*, see Needham 1956: 249)

Religious Taoism developed this idea, perhaps under the influence of Buddhism, into religious practices. One such practice is to buy living things which have been captured, such as fish, birds, or tortoises, and then to release them, in the belief that this kind of behaviour will definitely add to the agent's merit. In the Taoist book, *Lie Tzu*, of the third century CE, it is recorded that the people released 'the living things on New Year's Day as a gesture of kindness' (Graham 1960: 178). By the third and fourth centuries CE, protecting life had become one of the most important commandments, and is a necessary condition for becoming an immortal:

> For those people who seek immortality, their hearts must be kind to all things. They must treat others as they treat themselves and extend their love even to insects . . . Their hands must never injure life.
>
> (Ko Hung: *Pao-p'u Tzu*, see de Bary et al. 1960: 262)

However, the Taoist motive for abiding by this kind of commandment differs not only from that of Confucianism, but also from that of Buddhism. For Confucians, the protection of creatures is required for being in accordance with the *tao* of Heaven; for Buddhists, the interdict upon killing is connected with their conception of inter-transformation between human beings and other living beings, while, for Taoists, the first consideration is to reach immortality or to maintain a long life, and only from this consideration were derived the strong duties of protecting living things or forbidding the eating of meat. If a person killed a living thing, ate bloody meat, or even touched these unclean things, the gods residing in his or her body would feel disgusted and would therefore shorten his or her life, or even flee from the body, leading to death.

In folklore and popular religion, animals and birds also were imagined to have their own language and means of communication, and seem to have known more about nature than human beings. If humans happened to have the ability to understand their message, they might find a new world of knowledge, predicting possible changes in the cosmos and avoiding coming calamities. Besides animals, it is also widely believed that other creatures such as plants, flowers and trees also have spirits, and, like humans and animals, they can become gods and spiritual beings by obtaining the essence of Heaven and earth.

Compared with things, human beings have been generally given a higher value. Taoist masters list human beings as one of the 'Four Greatnesses of the Universe': *tao*, Heaven, Earth and Humanity (*Tao Te Ching* Chapter 25), while Confucianism thinks of human beings in the sense of moral righteousness:

> Water and fire have essences but not life; herbs and trees have life but not knowledge; birds and beasts have knowledge but no sense of what are rights [*yi*]; man has an essence, life, knowledge and in addition has a sense of rights. Hence he is the highest being on earth.
>
> (*Hsun Tzu*, see Dubs 1977: 136)

Things can be used to help to maintain their harmony; for this Chinese medicine and special religious rituals were invented. But, in the last analysis, there is no essential distinction between them. From this understanding, the oneness between humans and things is a necessary conclusion. In the Sung dynasty, a neo-Confucian, Chang Tsia, put this idea in a paragraph which has been regarded as the motto of this tradition:

> Heaven is my father and Earth is my mother . . . All people are my brothers and sisters, and all things are my companions.
>
> (See de Bary et al. 1960: 469)

Humanity is the microcosm of nature

In China, the popular religions flourished for a long time. On the one hand, these religious movements or practices borrowed a lot from the three established religions of Confucianism, Taoism and Buddhism. On the other hand, they independently used *yin-yang* and the Five Elements theories to explain almost everything. Therefore, we can know their fundamental attitude to nature by exploring these theories.

The universe is composed of two powers or principles, *yin* and *yang*. *Yin* and *yang* were used widely to represent two opposite and complementary extremes of nature: *yang* means day, sun, heaven, fire, heat, dryness, light, male, above, outer, and so on; *yin* means night, moon, earth, water, cold, dampness, dark, female, below, inner, and so on. They were also used to represent two principles which govern the universe; one is strong, active or masculine, the other is weak, non-active or feminine. These two extremes do not exclude each other but are complementary. The balance of *yin* and *yang* is the basis of cosmic harmony; as soon as this harmony is obstructed or destroyed, disaster will occur. In nature, in the state, in the family, and within the human body, to keep *yin* and *yang* in proper balance is the only way to retain well-being and to prosper.

Just as the ancient Greek philosophers used water, fire, air, earth, and other elements to describe the basis of the whole world, the ancient Chinese employed the theory of Five Elements (Five Agents,

Five Powers or Forces) to explain the structure and process of movement of the cosmos. The Five Elements are metal, wood, water, fire and earth. They connected closely not only with *yin* and *yang*, but with directions, colours and other things. Tung Chung-shu (?179–?104 BCE) explained this as:

> The vital forces of Heaven and earth join to form a unity, divide to become the yin and yang, separate into the four seasons, and range themselves into the Five Agents (Elements). 'Agent' in this case means activity.
>
> (See de Bary et al. 1960: 202)

Basically, there are two orders of the Five Elements. One is the order of their mutual producing: wood produces fire, fire produces earth, earth produces metal, metal produces water, and water produces wood. According to Tung Chung-shu, this can be compared to a sort of father and son relationship; as transmitters they are fathers, and as receivers they are sons. The second is the order of their mutual conquest: each element will give way to or be taken over by others – that is, wood conquers earth, metal conquers wood, fire conquers metal, water conquers fire and earth conquers water.

Yin-yang and the Five Elements carry themselves into human nature, life and morality. Within the body there is a system of *yin-yang* and the Five Elements. Corresponding to the Five Elements, there are five inner organs – liver, heart, lungs, kidneys and spleen. Liver is wood, and the representative of love and benevolence (*ren*). Lungs are metal, corresponding to righteousness. Heart is fire and keeps all things in their own order, and therefore is like propriety. The kidneys are water, and are like wisdom. The spleen is earth and is the zenith of trustfulness. It is quite obvious that, in the minds of the ancient Chinese, human organs, senses, and even moral character, were all generated by the interaction between *yin* and *yang* together with the combinations of the Five Elements. Clearly, human beings are the microcosm reflecting the macrocosm of the universe.

In nature, there originally was a harmony between *yin* and *yang*, and the right order among the Five Elements, but, due to the inappropriate activities of human beings, this harmony and order kept being broken or violated. The disorder in nature and the violation of the harmonious relation between humans and nature are fundamental causes of social chaos and individual suffering. Therefore, in order to maintain the proper order or to rebuild the harmony in the cosmos, a great variety of popular religious practices and beliefs appeared. *Feng shui* (geomancy) is just one of them. *Feng* means wind, *shui* means water, and these two words have been used to refer to all human environments or surroundings. The aims of *feng shui* are, in its best sense, to search for patterns of nature and decide how human beings should react to them; to find out what is the original harmonious state and suggest how humans could return to this state; to look for the flow and channel of *chi* governing the universe and human bodies and advise what might be done so as to strengthen human physical and spiritual power; and, lastly, to improve or to obtain good fortunes by maintaining the harmony between *yin* and *yang* and among the Five Elements (Needham 1956: 359–63).

Conclusion

In summary, the basic attitudes to nature in Chinese religion are that human beings come from nature, grow in nature and will return to nature. Nature not only provides the necessary conditions for living, but also is the model and best pattern for human life. Only that life which accords with nature is a good life. Violating the natural law leads to bad fortune and doom.

The value of this tradition has been rediscovered by contemporary eco-ethicists, and regarded as a representation of deep Asian wisdom (Callicot 1987). However, we have to point out that the concepts of *tao*, Heaven, 'ten thousand things', *yin-yang* and the Five Elements in Chinese tradition do not express exactly the same meaning as 'nature' in western culture. These concepts have been made somewhat mystical, and the unification between that to which they refer and human beings is, at most, a kind of religious experience rather than a scientific system. In addition, it must also be said that the attitudes to nature described above, for a long time in history, unfortunately have failed to be carried into the practice of the secular community in Chinese society.

FURTHER READING

Callicot, J. Baird (1987) 'Conceptual Resources for Eastern Philosophies in Asian Traditions of Thought: A Propaedeutic', *Philosophy East and West*, 37: 115–131.

de Bary, Wm. Theodore, Chan, Wing-Tsit and Watson, Burton (eds) (1960) *Sources of Chinese Tradition*, New York, Columbia University Press.

Dubs, Homer H. (trans.) (1977) *The Works of Hsuntse*, London, A. Probsthain.

Fung, Yu-lan (1952–53) *A History of Chinese Philosophy*, Volume I and Volume II, trans. Derk Bodde, London, Allen and Unwin.

Graham, A.C. (trans.) (1960) *The Book of Lieh-tzu*, London, John Murray.

Lau, D.C. (trans.) (1970) *Mencius*, London, Penguin.

Maspero, Henri (1981) *Taoism and Chinese Religion*, translated by Frank A. Kierman Jr, Amherst, University of Massachusetts Press.

Munro, Donald J. (1969) *The Concept of Man in Early China*, Stanford, Stanford University Press.

Needham, Joseph (1956) *Science and Civilization in China*, Volume 2, Cambridge, Cambridge University Press.

Watson, Burton (trans.) (1968) *The Complete Works of Chuang Tzu*, New York, Columbia University Press.

Wilhelm, Richard (1968) *I Ching*, trans. C.F. Baynes, London, Routledge and Kegan Paul.

8. Japanese Religions

Brian Bocking

A study of Japanese attitudes to nature must begin with a few words about our current attitudes to Japan and Japanese people. Images of Japan probably include ideas about martial arts, and an impression that the Japanese follow Buddhism and Shinto, two religions which teach peaceful co-existence with nature. At the same time, the Japanese are known worldwide for their advanced technology and business success, and some claim the Japanese are 'eco-terrorists' because they eat whales and are accused of deforesting Southeast Asia. Whales have become a symbol of the beauty, grandeur and fragility of the natural world, and in the battle to save the whale, the Japanese seem to have become the enemy. Our image of the Japanese, therefore, contains at least two contradictory pictures: a rather positive image of a disciplined and religious people living in harmony with nature, and a negative image of a business army prepared to plunder the earth's natural resources in pursuit of economic growth. In the context of these mixed perceptions, it is not surprising that in 1991 the Japanese Government set up a four-year research project involving over a hundred historians, archaeologists and specialists in economics, sociology and ecology, to establish what exactly are the differences between Japanese and western attitudes to nature (Ishi 1992: 2).

Are there 'eastern' and 'western' attitudes to nature?

According to Hiroyuki Ishi, a Japanese environmentalist and member of the research project on attitudes to nature, western and eastern attitudes developed out of two different patterns of agriculture, summed up as 'wheat and meat' in the West, and 'rice and fish' in the East. For example, in the West forests were always looked upon, in Ishi's words, as 'targets for development'. As land used for crops or grazing gradually became infertile, huge areas of forest were felled to provide new farmland. This led eventually to deforestation on a massive scale, especially in Mediterranean areas where western agriculture first began and where forests and topsoil have almost completely disappeared.

In Southeast Asia, by contrast, rice cultivation in paddy fields (artificial swamps) became the dominant mode of food production. Paddies are mainly constructed on flat or gently sloping land, so rice-growing is less likely to destroy hillside forests. Rice cultivation, moreover, relies on forests to soak up the rainwater flooding down from the mountains, and rice paddies can remain fertile for thousands of years. According to Ishi (1992: 3), 'great care was taken to ensure the availability of water, and forests, which acted as "green dams", were carefully protected. The protection of forests as a means of securing water resources has been a major concern in Japan throughout its history'. In Japan's Edo period (1600–1868) severe penalties were prescribed for people caught damaging trees – a finger was cut off for stealing a twig, an arm for a branch, and beheading for cutting down a tree. 'Records from the time show that large numbers of people suffered the ultimate penalty for stealing trees' (Ishi, 1992: 2–3).

On the controversial subject of whaling, Ishi observes that whales, though technically mammals, were traditionally thought of as fish by the Japanese, and fish were (and are) an important element in the Japanese diet. By contrast, the slaughtering of land animals such as cows and sheep, an accepted feature of traditional western societies, was frowned upon in Japan by both Buddhism (which tends to vegetarianism) and Shinto (which regards blood and death as polluting). Meat production in Japan was surrounded by taboos, and restricted to outcaste social groups (which have traditionally existed in Japan, as in India). Following the western example, introduced in the late nineteenth century, meat is now commonly eaten in Japan, and the flat northern island of Hokkaido, opened up to Japanese agriculture a century ago, is cattle-rearing country. Inhibitions about meat-eating have virtually disappeared now that meat is widely available.

Much more recently, the attitude of Japanese people towards whales has changed quite dramatically. A survey in 1991 showed that sixty-three per cent of Japanese respondents now regarded whales as wild animals deserving of protection, while thirty-three per cent thought whales were a source of food that could be hunted. The Japanese pro-whaling lobby had called for Japan to withdraw from the International Whaling Commission (the body which banned commercial whaling in 1982) but seventy-one per cent of Japanese people in the survey disagreed with this stance, although twenty-two per cent supported it. 'Whale watching' is now catching on as a leisure activity in Japan, so there has been a clear shift in attitudes to whales in Japan, as part of a general and worldwide change in consciousness of 'environmental' issues.[1]

These very recent changes in attitude, however, seem to show up the extent to which Japanese attitudes to nature seem to be *similar* to, rather than different from, 'western' attitudes. Japanese forests were protected, not because the Japanese had a particular reverence for trees as such, but because forests were necessary to the success of crops. As rice cultivation in Japan has decreased in recent years, disused paddy fields and associated forests have fallen into decay. In addition, concern for the preservation of forests has not extended to Japanese operations in other countries in Southeast Asia, where massive and unsustainable logging operations are providing wood for the Japanese construction industry and other purposes. Westerners have preserved forests when they wanted to (e.g. for hunting), and westerners too used to catch and process whales without any special affection for them or any regard for the eventual environmental impact of high-tech whaling. Like the Japanese, people in the West conventionally class whales as fish because they swim in the sea, and westerners have had inhibitions about eating some land animals, as well-known dietary laws in Islam and Judaism, and customary taboos on eating dogs or, in the UK, horses, demonstrate. Westerners were using whale products until very recently when the whale became, first an endangered species, and then a symbol of the ecosystem. Can we really accept that there is a difference between western 'wheat and meat' and eastern 'rice and fish' attitudes to nature?

Differences between 'western' and 'Japanese' attitudes to nature might not lie so much in different forms of food production, as in different understandings of what 'nature' means, and hence of what our responsibilities towards 'nature' are. Modern western attitudes to nature derive from the religious traditions of Judaism, Christianity and Islam, which share, broadly speaking, the same model of the relationship between humans and the natural world. On this model, God created the world for human beings. Nature is fundamentally different from the human world – for example, animals do not have souls – and nature is there mainly to feed, clothe and shelter human beings, who have a responsibility to manage it well. A 'responsible' attitude here implies one which puts the interests of all human beings in the world first.

Modern environmental consciousness can be seen as a new, quasi-religious doctrine of the western type. The 'religion' of environmentalism emphasises the wonder of the creation, contrasts this with the alienation and folly of humans which need urgently to be replaced by reconciliation and wisdom, and looks forward either to a 'saved' (ecologically balanced) world or to the hell of an environmental armageddon if we do not repent of our ways. Within this 'religion', the whale has become a central symbol of the faith, an icon to distinguish the believer from the unbeliever, the responsibly minded from the irresponsible.

Japanese religion

How does this western-style 'religion of environmentalism', with its emphasis on our responsibility to nature and warnings about the future, fit, if at all, with Japanese attitudes to nature? Japanese attitudes and patterns of thinking are not derived from Judaism, Islam or Christianity, though there are, of course, Japanese adherents of these faiths today. The Japanese world view was formed over 1500 years by the interaction of Taoism, Confucianism, Buddhism and Shinto. Taoism and Confucianism came from China; Buddhism originated in India and entered Japan from China through Korea; Shinto (originally a collective term for innumerable local religions) originated in Japan. These religions form in the Japanese mind a variegated single tradition which we can call 'Japanese religion', whose chief characteristics are as follows:

1. Japanese religion is local, not universal. The Japanese do not feel responsible for the salvation of the whole world. They do feel a very strong responsibility for others in their own social group, such as their own family, community, or sometimes nation.

2. Humans can live happily in the world. Japanese religion does not consider human beings to be intrinsically sinful, as 'cast out' into the world. Problems occur in the world but they are not a punishment or consequence of original sin. Problems are just problems, and have to be dealt with in a matter-of-fact way.
3. The world comprises different kinds of beings, such as spirits, gods, humans, ancestors, animals, fish, trees and rocks. Human beings are part of the flow of things (the *tao*) and have no particular responsibilities over and above other kinds of beings.
4. Japanese religion does not expect the end of the world, when those who are right will be saved and the rest destroyed. The future will probably be very much like the present in all important respects. Nothing that humans do is going to bring about the end of the world.
5. Religious practice is a private affair. It is accepted that different groups within society will develop a relationship with different symbols and objects of faith (as in Hinduism). There are no religious symbols which everyone ought to revere, and no single 'right' religion.
6. Japanese life has always been, and still is, permeated by the Confucian ethic, which puts social harmony and the well-being of the group (rather than individual rights) at the heart of morality. This means that a 'responsible' attitude is one which conforms to the views and values of one's immediate social group (e.g., the family, or one's company). A person who thinks or acts in ways which undermine the group consensus is seen as weak and unreliable. A 'group ethic' approach is not unique to Japan; it is found in many traditional societies and in sub-groups within advanced industrial nations (such as the Freemasons in the UK, or the Mafia in the USA). However, Japan is an advanced industrialised society with a great deal of economic influence in the world, and mainstream Japanese society is based on a group-centred morality. This kind of morality disturbs those who claim to hold 'universal' moral values. However, in practice the more 'universal' a value-system is, the more likely it is that informal sub-systems will develop within it to give priority to the interests of certain groups, such as nations.

In the light of these six characteristics of the traditional Japanese world view, what can we expect Japanese attitudes to nature and the environment to look like?

JAPANESE RELIGION IS LOCAL, NOT UNIVERSAL

For the ordinary Japanese person, 'nature' means the local, rather than the world, environment. Japanese people, as the whaling survey mentioned at the beginning of this chapter showed, are well able to think globally on issues such as whaling, but they are unlikely to do so unless (a) global matters are shown to have local implications, and (b) attention to global issues does not divert attention from local concerns, which are automatically seen as more important than distant matters. Once an issue is accepted as belonging to the local community (which may often these days be 'Japan'), the Japanese can move with extraordinary speed to remedy the situation, and will strive to achieve a consensus in order to make radical changes if necessary. On the other hand, environmental destruction happening abroad tends to be regarded as 'not our problem' until a connection with Japan is established.

HUMANS CAN LIVE HAPPILY IN THE WORLD

The Japanese have a strong sense of belonging within a natural world which can be a comfortable, beautiful and enjoyable place. According to Japanese thinking, human perfection is possible, though occasionally things go out of balance. When things go well, one can just enjoy life. When things go badly, one does one's best to set things straight. Floods, earthquakes and typhoons are regular occurrences in Japan, but nature also sustains us and instructs us. Most Japanese are not impressed by the claim that we need to be saved from this world, and consequently are not easily persuaded that the world needs to be saved from us! To the Japanese mind, human beings and nature are equally at home with each other. This affinity is expressed in the Shinto notion of *kami*, and in Zen Buddhism, which has strong affinities with Chinese Taoism.

THE WORLD COMPRISES DIFFERENT KINDS OF BEINGS

It is a conceit, to the Japanese mind, to think that humans have superior rights over other kinds of beings. Ancestors are a case in point. Traditional Japanese attitudes to ancestral spirits suggest that life is seen as a 'repayment' to ancestors (parents, grandparents, et al.) for bringing us into the world and giving us education, sustenance and opportunities. This should be repaid with care and reverential treatment. In the same way, human beings are indebted to nature (often personified in the notion of *kami*, sacred energies or spirits who inhere in natural phenomena) for the nourishment and shelter nature provides. Dore (1967) asked a hundred Japanese city dwellers the question: 'People say that we are the recipients of *on* [favours which require repayment] from the moment that we come into this world. What do you think?' Among the varied replies was one from a man who said, 'I can't say directly, but, for instance, when the weather clears after a long spell of rain, somehow you feel as if you want to thank somebody'.[2]

The model is one of reciprocity between different sorts of being, rather than stewardship of a resource. There are some disgruntled ancestors and spirits, who can be dealt with if necessary through religious practice, but there are also helpful spirits and benign ancestors. There is no Prince of Darkness sowing evil in the world, and the Japanese feel that human nature, far from being innately sinful and corrupt, is a perfectly adequate measure of right and wrong.

JAPANESE RELIGION DOES NOT EXPECT THE END OF THE WORLD

In keeping with its broadly optimistic view of human nature and the world, Japanese religion does not anticipate a cataclysm. On the contrary, Japanese religion tends to be rather nostalgic – looking back to a time when things were in balance and reciprocal relationships between humans, gods and nature were untroubled, and seeking to restore that balance. The idea that, if we get it wrong now, a final judgement will fall upon us, is simply alien to Japanese consciousness; it is not found in any of the religions which have contributed to the Japanese world view. The threat of global environmental disaster, therefore, seems far more familiar and convincing to those who are influenced by western religious thought-patterns than it does to the ordinary Japanese.

RELIGIOUS BELIEFS ARE A PRIVATE AFFAIR

Despite the emphasis on behavioural conformity in Japanese society, the influence of Buddhism, which teaches that there are many paths to the goal of enlightenment, and the example of Shinto, which celebrates the presence and power of the *kami* in an astonishing variety of local ways, have meant that the Japanese are used to living with a multiplicity of religious beliefs and practices, including different religious symbols and objects of devotion. Such objects of devotion (for example, a particular named *buddha* or *kami*) do not have the same universal meaning in Japan as an image of Jesus, say, might have in the West.

In the case of 'environmental religion', Japanese people can readily understand that some people wish to refrain from killing any whales at all, for quasi-religious reasons (namely, that the whale symbolises for those people fragile nature). Most find it difficult to grasp why those who are not devotees of the 'way of the whale' should also be expected to refrain from killing or eating a few whales. Religious tolerance, which has been greatly valued in Japan when governments have allowed it (as at present), implies a 'live and let live' attitude to various truth-claims. This is frustrating to missionaries of any universalist gospel.

THE CONFUCIAN ETHIC PUTS SOCIAL HARMONY AND THE WELL-BEING OF THE GROUP (RATHER THAN INDIVIDUAL RIGHTS) AT THE HEART OF MORALITY

Finally, the Japanese attitude to nature must be put into context as part of a Confucian world view. Confucianism evaluates things according to their effect on the social group. A person, animal, field or forest is either *uchi* (ours – literally 'inside') or *soto* (not ours – literally 'outside'). Nature, in the sense of wild life and uncultivated tracts of land, is not, in traditional Japanese thought, *uchi*. Remote forests and mountains in Japan are dangerous, 'other' places, the haunt of strange beings such as the half-human, half-bird *tengu*,[3] and suitable only for Buddhist or Shinto ascetic practices.

To the Japanese way of thinking, any humans, animals, crops and forests which are 'inside' (*uchi*), in the sense of belonging to 'my' social world, have an absolute claim to my protection and support. However, that part of the human and natural world which falls 'outside' (*soto*) 'my' social world or group is, emphatically, not my responsibility. Thus a 'responsible' person in Japanese terms is one who fulfils all obligations within the group – the *uchi* context – but also recognises the precise limits of responsibility and does not seek to interfere in 'outside' areas.

Conclusion

In summary, contemporary western attitudes to nature derive from 'universal' values, which are really values applying to the group of all human beings in the world. In order to safeguard the interests of the group of human beings, 'nature', which is defined as anything outside the human realm, must be properly managed. If not, the mismanagement of nature will bring about the well-deserved destruction of humankind (which those in the West are conditioned by their religious heritage to expect).

Japanese attitudes to 'nature' define nature in a different way, to mean 'the world enjoyably inhabited by our social group'. Within this world, there are natural, human and supernatural elements. These interact, and get out of balance when proper reciprocity is not observed. Imbalance can be corrected by recognising that something we are doing is having an adverse effect on 'our' group, and then acting decisively, using our group's wisdom, to remedy it. This may involve redefining 'our' group to include elements previously thought not to be part of 'us' (such as activities done on our behalf in other countries). The world is not going to come to a cataclysmic end – that would damage our group – so we will assess the situation, reach a consensus and then take the necessary steps to avoid a cataclysm.

NOTES

1. The survey is discussed by Ishi, H. (1992) pp. 7, 11. Ishi notes that when respondents in the USA, the (former) USSR and Japan were

recently asked to list the issues that concerned them most, the Japanese chose the environment first, while environment came third in the other countries. Ishi concludes (p. 11) that 'public opinion [in Japan] is changing ahead of government policy'.

2. Dore R. (1967), p. 371
3. For a description of the *tengu* (and an encounter with one) see Carmen Blacker (1975) pp. 182–5.

FURTHER READING

Blacker, C. (1975) *The Catalpa Bow; a Study of Shamanistic Practices in Japan*, London, George Allen and Unwin.

Bocking, B. (1987) 'The Japanese Religious Traditions in Today's World', in Whaling, F. (ed.), *Religion in Today's World*, Edinburgh, T & T Clark.

Davis, W. (1992) *Japanese Religion and Society*, Albany, State University of New York Press.

Dore, R. (1967) *City Life in Japan*, Berkeley and Los Angeles, University of California Press.

Earhart, H.B. (1974) *Religion in the Japanese Experience: Sources and Interpretations*, Encino, California, Dickenson Publishing Company.

Hori, I. (ed.) (1981) *Japanese Religion*, Tokyo, Kodansha.

Ishi, H. (1992) 'Attitudes Toward the Natural World and the Whaling Issue', *The Japan Foundation Newsletter*, Vol. XIX, No. 4: 1–7, 11.

Ono, S. (1962) *Shinto: the Kami Way*, Rutland Vermont, Tuttle.

Reader, I. (1991) *Religion in Contemporary Japan*, London, Macmillan.

Reid, D. (1984) 'Japanese Religions', in Hinnells, J.R. (ed.) *Handbook of Living Religions*, Harmondsworth, Penguin.

Index